"Jean Jenson's approach helps the adult to mourn the losses of childhood without at the same time losing himself in the chaos of his own feelings. . . . For a person caught up in the chaos of his feelings, Jean Jenson's book provides aid in structuring that chaos . . . if the need is there, the person in question cannot but profit from Jenson's clear, detailed guidance. . . . In clear, simple language, with an abundance of examples, Jenson gives her readers the chance to find their own way to their own truth and at the same time maintain a receptive attitude toward anything new which they may come across and which can be of help to them."

—from the New Foreword by Alice Miller

"Reflects a wealth of clinical understanding that is too often not present in self-help books. One cannot fail to appreciate the depth of her sensitivity, empathy, and respect for children raised in an atmosphere of neglect and abuse. Rather than merely listing symptoms, Jenson honors strength and resiliency and invites her readers to see themselves in others with compassion and respect while she guides them on a clearly marked path that shows that healing is possible. This is an excellent book not to be missed by anyone who has been affected by a painful childhood or anyone working with children or adult survivors of childhood abuse and neglect."

—Jane Middleton, Author of *Shame and Guilt,
Children of Trauma,* and *Will to Survive*

JEAN JENSON, M.S.W., is a psychotherapist with nearly thirty years of experience in the field of mental health, fifteen of them in private practice. This is her first book. She lives in Hailey, Idaho.

ALICE MILLER, a practicing psychotherapist for over twenty years, is the author of bestselling, pioneering books on child abuse and its effects, including *The Drama of the Gifted Chid, Thou Shalt Not Be Aware,* and *Breaking Down the Wall of Silence* (the last two available in Meridian editions).

D0047718

JEAN C. JENSON, M.S.W.

reclaiming your life

A Step-by-Step Guide

to Using Regression

Therapy to Overcome

the Effects of Childhood Abuse

New Foreword by Alice Miller

A MERIDIAN BOOK

MERIDIAN
Published by Penguin Group
Penguin Group (USA) Inc., 375 Hudson Street, New York, New York 10014, U.S.A.
Penguin Group (Canada), 90 Eglinton Avenue East, Suite 700, Toronto, Ontario, Canada M4P 2Y3
(a division of Pearson Penguin Canada Inc.)
Penguin Books Ltd., 80 Strand, London WC2R 0RL, England
Penguin Ireland, 25 St. Stephen's Green, Dublin 2, Ireland (a division of Penguin Books Ltd.)
Penguin Group (Australia), 250 Camberwell Road, Camberwell, Victoria 3124, Australia
(a division of Pearson Australia Group Pty. Ltd.)
Penguin Books India Pvt. Ltd., 11 Community Centre, Panchsheel Park, New Delhi – 110 017, India
Penguin Group (NZ), 67 Apollo Drive, Rosedale, North Shore 0745, Auckland, New Zealand
(a division of Pearson New Zealand Ltd.)
Penguin Books (South Africa) (Pty.) Ltd., 24 Sturdee Avenue, Rosebank, Johannesburg 2196, South Africa

Penguin Books Ltd., Registered Offices: 80 Strand, London WC2R 0RL, England

Published by Meridian, a member of Penguin Group (USA) Inc. Previously published in a Dutton edition.

First Meridian Printing, October 1996
20 19 18 17 16 15

Copyright © Jean C. Jenson, 1995
Foreword copyright © Alice Miller, 1996
All rights reserved

 REGISTERED TRADEMARK—MARCA REGISTRADA

The Library of Congress has catalogued the Dutton edition as follows:

Jenson, Jean C.
    Reclaiming your life: a step-by-step guide to using regression therapy to overcome the effects of childhood
abuse/Jean C. Jenson:
    foreword by Alice Miller.
        p.   cm.
    Includes bibliographical references and index.
    ISBN 0-525-93948-2 (h.c.)
    ISBN 978-0-452-01169-4 (pbk.)
    1. Adult child abuse victims–Rehabilitation.   2. Regression (Psychology)–Therapeutic use.   3. Catharsis.
4. Self-help techniques.   I. Title.
RC569.5.C55J46   1995
616.85'822390651–dc20
                                                                                                94-34390

Printed in the United States of America
Original hardcover design by Steven N. Stathakis

This book is dedicated
to my daughter, Emily,
whose presence blesses
my life.

Contents

Foreword to the
Meridian Edition
by Alice Miller

It is more than twenty years now since I made the discovery that pictures I had painted spontaneously were a source of revelation about my own past, a discovery that inspired me to start writing about the effects of childhood traumas on our lives as adults. For some time I believed that primal therapy could provide the key to working through these old wounds. Finally, however, I came to see that working on the past is something that can be achieved only by the *adult* part of the personality, not by the child. Regression to the stage of early infancy is not a suitable method in and of itself. Such a regression can only be effective if it happens in the natural course of therapy and if the client is able to maintain adult consciousness at the same time.

Jean Jenson's approach reflects her obvious awareness of this fact. It helps the adult to mourn the losses of childhood without at the same time losing herself in the chaos of her own feelings. In the seventies Jean Jenson experienced primal therapy in operation at Arthur Janov's institute. Later, however, she went on to develop a therapy design that, in the all-important question of regression and the understanding of what actually happens in the therapeutic process, represents a notable advance on that particular method.

To what extent readers will be able to employ this method without expert assistance remains to be seen. My present view is that the assistance of a therapist with the necessary competence and integrity is essential if the client is to be able to develop her capacity for change to the fullest. To exploit the entire range of her potential for growth, a potential stunted in childhood by neglect or cruelty, she must be in the presence of someone perceptive, affirmative, and protective and who will not try to take advantage of her.

Jean Jenson may indeed have succeeded in reducing the dangers of primal therapy to a minimum while at the same time enhancing its positive aspects. Time will tell. In her much discussed book *Therapy Gone Mad* (1984), Carol L. Mithers draws upon a number of extreme cases to demonstrate the dangers that can arise through exploitation of regression. Perhaps *Reclaiming Your Life* can help reduce these dangers.

For a person caught up in the chaos of his feelings, Jean Jenson's book provides aid in structuring that chaos. With the help of her exercises the adult can learn to work on the feelings that go back to his childhood and to distinguish between the two levels—the child's consciousness and the adult's reality (see Chapter 3).

Aided by this distinction, he is able to identify and exploit the opportunities that his present life offers him without reverting to the helplessness of a child and thus laying himself wide open to potential manipulation. In so doing he creates for himself the possibility of a self-induced, structured regression into the past undertaken in the service of a process of maturity—*if* this is what he wants and needs. I feel that this latter question is one that requires very careful consideration before the decision is taken to embark on such an experiment. By no means does everyone feel the need to explore their own childhood, certainly not to the extent that I myself did. But if the need is there, the person in question cannot but profit from Jenson's clear, detailed guidance.

Today I know that a method that is successful for one person will not necessarily be successful for another. This applies to all methods, and primal therapy is no exception. Some people insist that it saved their lives; others say that they got nothing out of it, that in fact it did them considerable harm. Then again there are people who have benefited from therapy without being confronted with the past at all. The reasons for this have only recently become clear to me. If therapy succeeds in creating a basis for encouraging psychic growth, then the client is able to develop the ability both to perceive her own needs and to satisfy them. This reduces the impact of early neglect on the present life of the client. Traumas lose their significance once therapy is successful in helping us to shape our own lives more satisfactorily and to make our own independent decisions. Anyone subjected as a child to cruelty of whatever kind will indeed be impaired or handicapped in her ability to do this. But confrontation with past suffering will not automatically set that ability free.

What some of the cases described by Jenson demonstrate very graphically is that painful experiences from the past frequently have an alarming impact if present needs are neglected, ignored, not taken seriously, or unknown because one is still feeling like a helpless, dependent child.

Without an understanding that one is an adult with present needs, confrontation with the past can flood the patient's consciousness with the overwhelming childhood reality, and the goal of the experience then becomes to survive all over again. No understanding relating to present, adult reality is gained, and new "alarms" make it necessary to repeatedly relive the initial trauma in an addictive way. But if in therapy present needs are recognized, articulated, and taken seriously so that they can be satisfied as completely as possible, then important prerequisites for a sound further development have been achieved, and the patient can free himself more easily from the snares of the past, regardless of the therapeutic method used. Expecting that one day complete and permanent release from the consequences of childhood traumas will be feasible via primal therapy is rather unrealistic and can also generate unnecessary stress by subjecting patients to the strain of trying for goals that may be unattainable.

Jenson's model appears to me to be both easy to use and easy to evaluate. The author does not inflict any moralizing or pedagogic claims on her readers; she never implies that her recommendations are the supreme and ultimate wisdom on this matter or that she alone has the key to the problem. It is the honesty of her intentions that stands out. In clear, simple language, with an abundance of examples, Jenson gives her readers the chance to find their own way to their own truth and at the same time maintain a receptive attitude toward anything new which they may come across and which can be of help to them. This is a good thing. Until recently, traditional psychology had little time for feelings. With major interest suddenly being taken in emotions, thanks not least to modern neurobiological research, we can expect many new and exciting developments in the near future.

(Translated by Andrew Jenkins)

Acknowledgments

My gratitude to my friend Premi Pearson is more than I can express. First, she was willing to share her editorial skills, which are considerable. Her ability to grasp the writer's meaning and find ways to say it better for the reader's understanding, as well as her thorough knowledge of correct forms of expression, were invaluable to me. More than this, she freely gave time, which is precious to her, to pay attention to me when I needed encouragement and the support of an exchange of ideas. This book would not have been possible without her.

Similarly, there is no "thanks" big enough to acknowledge Alice Miller's involvement in calling this book to the attention of the publisher. She is truly an amazing woman—willing not only to read my manuscript just because I asked her to but to expend an enormous amount of time and energy in the effort.

My gratitude is also extended to Sally McCollum, Ph.D., for being willing—on short notice—to review much of the manuscript. Her input was especially valuable because of her thorough under-

standing of the various theoretical frameworks upon which psychotherapy has traditionally been based.

My thanks, too, to Jon Thorson for originally introducing me to
Alice Miller's works, for his suggestion that I read Miller's *Banished Knowledge*, for reading my manuscript and offering detailed
comments, and for numerous other ways of supporting me in this
project. I also want to thank Linda O'Shea, Jon's life partner, for the
continued encouragement she offered throughout the project.

Two people who may be surprised to find their names listed
here are included because their words, although expressed a few
years ago, have since echoed in my mind, nudging me to write this
book: Julie Lawson, with a small smile on her face, saying "What's
stopping you from writing that book, Jean, are you afraid?" and
Mike Martin, who also offered to help in any way he could, saying
"You've got something to say! Say it!"

My good friends Anne Pemberton and Kim Slayton have my
gratitude for the way in which each helped me, always at the right
time and in the right way.

Thanks also to my writer friend Mary Clare Griffin for the advice she offered, especially when I didn't know I needed it.

Finally, there is a man whose name I don't know who approached me after a presentation I gave in Pocatello, Idaho, as part
of a daylong "inner child" conference. He said, "I am a workshop
junky, and your material is the most helpful I have ever heard. You
must write a book." It was his comment that gave me the final push
I needed, and this book is written around the workshop I presented
that day. So, whoever you are, thank you.

reclaiming
your life

Introduction

I am a clinical social worker with almost thirty years' experience in the field of mental health. I have spent the last fourteen years in private practice, counseling adults and couples. The focus of my therapy is to help clients resolve childhood experiences that are still interfering with their lives.

My interest in becoming a psychotherapist grew out of my attempt to improve the quality of my own life through therapy. The "dysfunctional family" experience I had was of a more subtle nature than many—the damage was more a result of what didn't happen than what did—involving limits to my parents' ability to properly nurture all their children, especially in the years following my birth.

Because of these subtleties—I was not beaten, nor was I generally shouted at—it took me a long time to understand how my childhood had influenced me. Only after spending years as a client using traditional therapies did I discover how to uncover previously unconscious experiences. Then I really understood how and why childhood experiences were still interfering with my adult life. By this time, I had obtained a master's degree in social work, originally intending to work with groups of young people through a social service agency, the YWCA or YMCA, or community centers. Instead, I was influenced by my own therapy experiences to become a psychotherapist because I knew that the method I had learned was truly effective in helping people change.

When I established my private practice in Idaho fourteen years ago, most attempts at psychological self-help came in the form of large, weeklong or weekend encounter groups, "spiritual-growth" retreats led by famous mediators, or semisecret growth groups like Erhart Seminar Training. There were relatively few self-help books available. Most conventional psychotherapy was based on developmental theory; the role of the therapist was to help the client discover which developmental task had not been properly "mastered" in childhood so that the client could seek such mastery now, with the help of the therapist.

The early 1980s saw the emergence of the "adult child" movement. Adult Children of Alcoholics, which grew rapidly throughout the country, was based on the understanding that, even if not alcoholics themselves, adults who had been children in alcoholic families had suffered abuse and continued to experience lasting effects from it. In 1987 the nationwide First Annual Adult Children of Alcoholics (later Adult Children of Dysfunctional Families) Conference was held. These developments changed the public and professional thinking about the influence of abusive childhoods and about what abuse really is.

Now the concept that our childhoods do affect our adult lives has become more credible among the general population than ever before. For individuals recovering from substance abuse or addiction through 12-Step Programs (served by groups such as Alcoholics Anonymous and Narcotics Anonymous) and their families (served by Alanon and Alateen), therapists have developed concepts such as "co-dependency," the "adult child," and the "inner child," plus dozens of self-help books, residential treatment programs, conferences appealing to both mental health professionals and lay adult children, audio- and videotapes, television shows, etc.

The books, magazine articles, tapes, and conferences do a good job of demonstrating the nature and extent of childhood abuse in our culture. More and more people are now aware that abuse is not only physical, or sexual, but can be emotional and psychological as well. The term "denial," once the private preserve of psychotherapists, has become commonplace among those who have been educated by this deluge of resources.

After people began to understand and accept that many of us had abusive childhoods—and that the experiences we had as children were interfering with our ability to function optimally as adults—the next step was to decide what to do about it. Most authors and lecturers first focused on areas of dysfunction—the "issues"—that adult children had in common. These issues are typically "behaviors," often categorized as caretaking, low self-esteem, obsessiveness, dependence or antidependence, control, and denial. Thus, when we worry about whether an adult family member will remember to do something important, and we remind him or her (without having been asked to do so), we are caretaking and controlling. When we continue to worry about a problem after having done everything we can about it (especially if it's someone else's problem in the first place), when we respond with terrible anxiety to small mishaps, we are obsessing. When we are afraid of other people's anger or of making mistakes; when we feel as though we are not good enough; when we want to hide for fear of what people will think about us; when we feel guilty, angry, or defensive when questioned about something, we are exhibiting low self-esteem. When we act as though we can't do anything for ourselves without help or, conversely, when we strive to act as though we never need any help, we are acting either overly dependent or as if we had no dependency needs at all. These are all examples of the kinds of behaviors, destructive and self-defeating, that have been described as resulting from these adult child "issues."

Dozens of self-help books have been written to define the problem of, and offer solutions for, the emerging subgroup of adult children called "co-dependents," who repeatedly act to take care of others at the expense of their own well-being. Typically, solutions are based on recognizing abuse experiences in the family of origin, discovering "issues," becoming aware of self-destructive behaviors resulting from these issues, and learning to substitute healthy behaviors. Support groups, based on the 12-Step Program of Alcoholics Anonymous (AA), have become very popular as means to help people learn new, healthy behaviors. Such programs rely on help from a "higher power," the backbone of AA's original 12 Steps, to make that change possible.

The term "in recovery," long used by alcoholics and drug addicts who have stopped drinking and using, who are members of a 12-Step Program, and who live their lives by the 12 Steps, was adopted wholesale by the new 12-Step groups based on adult child or co-dependent identification. The concept that the alcoholic will always be alcoholic, whether "in recovery" or not, was also adopted. Adult children and co-dependents similarly accepted that they have a lifelong "disease" that is incurable, but by living with new, healthy behaviors, they will be "in recovery" from that "disease."

In my experience, applying the disease/recovery concept, which research supports as valid for alcoholics and other chemically dependent people, to nonaddicts suffering from the effects of abusive childhoods has taken the focus of treatment well past the points of similarity between the needs of these two populations. Such an exact application of the AA formula to this group is not only inappropriate but limits the potential for healing the past. Instead, it creates a belief that these people are afflicted with a condition that will require daily attention for the rest of their lives, as well as continued help from support groups. Such an approach deals largely with superficial results of unresolved childhood experiences, severely curtailing what is truly possible.

In the past six years, however, there has been a blossoming of awareness regarding the number of adults who come from families in which some kind of abuse was experienced as an ongoing part of the child-rearing practices. This awareness began with the population of recovering alcoholics and their families but has expanded to people from what has come to be called "dysfunctional families" (alcohol abuse being one kind of dysfunction). What began as basically a grassroots movement has influenced the counseling community as well, and more psychotherapists have begun to focus on childhood experiences in treating their clients.

For more than two decades, there has been an increasing dependence on cognitive-behavioral approaches. Practically speaking, this means that the therapist's goal has been to help clients consciously evaluate their lives and their behaviors, and learn to change self-defeating behaviors to more satisfying ones. With this influence already in operation, the focus for most psychotherapists working with the childhoods of their clients has been to follow the same pattern as previously described: to help their clients overcome denial, identify issues and the behaviors arising from them, then learn new, healthy behaviors and practice them. Often the model used to explain the origin of these unhealthy behaviors has been a learning one. It has been postulated, for instance, that one cannot learn healthy behaviors in an unhealthy family. Most of the therapeutic emphasis then, whether in support groups or psychotherapy, has been on relearning, sometimes called "reparenting."

Other therapists, like myself, have always worked with the concept that early, painful childhood experiences cannot be processed by the child, and that one function of our unconscious mind is to block our awareness of the full impact of these experiences. This blocking results in a kind of "storage" of repressed memories of which the individual is not consciously aware. It is this storage that causes the adult's problems; and the solution is to retrieve what has been stored in order to bring it to consciousness, where it can be examined and dealt with.

The 12-Step Programs used by Adult Children Anonymous (ACA) and Co-dependents Anonymous (CODA) may indeed be supportive group experiences. They may also teach the valuable spiritual lesson that events are not always within human control. But to apply the disease concept, accurate with regard to substance abusers and addicts, is a destructive mistake. Rather, it should be understood that the adult child population, and numerous unidentified others, are suffering from problems in their adult lives as a result of the *defenses* they needed to use as children to survive their abusive

families—not because they developed a disease. The behaviors that
are of concern are part of those old defenses, which must be dis-
mantled if change is to occur. Moreover, this dismantling must take
into account the experiences stored in the unconscious, and those
experiences are painful.

Like many recovering alcoholics who have felt that the 12-Step
Program was "not enough," adult children and co-dependents have
begun to feel something lacking. Somehow, their lives have not
changed as they expected them to. Somehow, they have not been
able to change their behaviors—even when they knew what they
were supposed to be doing. Such recognition has pointed to the
need to confront painful feelings rather than just learn new ways
to behave.

The growing recognition within the adult child and co-dependent
movement of the need to feel our childhood pain as part of the healing process instead of focusing on changing behavior is a welcome
step in the right direction. It is only a beginning, however, as even
authors and group leaders who are aware of the need to confront the
old, childhood pain don't really explain how this is to be accomplished. It's my impression that even the therapists, authors, and lecturers who understand the need to deal with the pain think that
talking about it, perhaps with some tears, is enough.

But "talking about" something is a conscious act, done by the
conscious mind, and it cannot help us deal with stored pain, which
is unconscious. Talking and crying while remembering is not
enough to achieve full resolution. Although it provides relief, it does
not provide healing.

As I learned through association with Arthur Janov* many years
ago, healing requires "regressive work"—regressing into childhood
experience, including the painful emotions to be found there—to
bring real, permanent healing. Much of the current information available to people seeking self-help guidance stops short of the final step.

---

*Some of the terminology found in this book that I find useful in describing regressive work was
originally used by Janov.

The necessary and final step is to understand what regression is, why it's needed in order to heal, and how to do it. This book is intended to provide the information needed to take that final step.

HOW TO USE THIS BOOK

I will present material on regression work as it relates to most of our daily lives and common experiences. It will be gradually "assembled," much as a house is built, from the foundation up. This approach is necessary because, although much of what motivates us is unconscious, we are not taught about our unconscious mind and how it operates. Most of us are not even taught that the unconscious exists, much less how it operates. My purpose, then, is to acquaint the reader with such new information so that it can be absorbed gradually. This approach may make the reader impatient—initially the material may appear to be overly simplistic or familiar—but it is important not to rush through it. It is essential to take time and read carefully and thoughtfully, remaining open to the ideas being discussed. Each chapter is a bridge leading to the next, and together they create the complete structure.

I have provided self-help exercises for the reader's guidance, and included case histories that describe the effects of doing the work, but these will be useful only for the reader who has first fully understood the material in the body of the book.

chapter one

Overreaction and Underreaction: The Consequences of Repression and Denial

Because her husband's salary alone does not provide enough income for the family, Jane has worked as a full-time clerk for a small insurance agency since the youngest of her three children started primary school several years ago. Her husband's job as manager of a local grocery store is a demanding one, requiring that he put in extra hours with little notice, so they both expected that Jane would continue to be responsible for most of the care of the household.

This proved very draining, and it was difficult for Jane to manage both her job and the family needs as well. After a while, Jane began to complain about it to the other women who worked in her office. She realized that she had never questioned her role as housewife because she liked it; indeed, she would have been happy to be able to be just a wife and mother.

But Jane also realized that she was in the habit of going along with things she *didn't* like, such as her husband's decisions on how the family vacations were spent. It had never before occurred to Jane that these things could be negotiated, with each of the family members having a voice. At the same time, she began to be aware of the fact that men in the office treated the women, including herself, differently than they treated each other. One man she didn't even like called her "honey," and she had been on the receiving end of looks and pats that felt more intrusive than friendly. Jane found herself discontented with a lot of things that she had not even noticed before, but she didn't know how to change them.

In discussing these concerns with her friends at work, Jane learned about Adult Children Anonymous (ACA) and Co-dependents Anonymous (CODA). One friend told Jane that these were groups for people from "dysfunctional families," and although she wasn't quite sure what that meant, Jane did know that she was always in conflict with her mother, who seemed stubbornly self-destructive about caring properly for herself. She went to a few meetings with her friend and liked it.

Jane has now attended ACA or CODA meetings on a weekly basis for over a year and has read a good number of self-help books on co-dependency and dysfunctional families. She has learned how to tell her husband that she doesn't want to go sport fishing on their vacations or see his family every Christmas and that the children should have a say in it also (setting limits); she no longer allows her office mate to put his arm round her shoulders and give her a squeeze without permission (establishing boundaries); she has stopped making several phone calls each year to "get" her mother to have a mammogram (refusing to accept responsibilities that aren't hers); and she has established a program whereby everyone in the family shares household management so she is no longer doing all the housework as well as being employed full-time. Still, Jane does not feel the happiness that she thought these changes would bring. Something is missing.

Jane still feels hurt, angry, resentful, left out, afraid of saying or even thinking certain things. She cannot just relax and read a book or go for a walk. She still "puts herself down," feels like an inadequate wife and mother, and wonders if she's doing a good enough job at work. She thinks she is sometimes mean to her husband and kids and that she should have better control over her temper, two things that seemed to develop along with her new understandings.

Jane also worries about her relationship with her parents. They are getting older, and she finds it difficult to want to go "home" to see them. A couple of years ago, when she first started going to ACA meetings, she realized they had not been very good parents to her, and she felt angry for a while. Then she read some books and did some work on "forgiveness." She felt really good after she was able to forgive them. But, somehow, she is still very uncomfortable with her parents, even when they call to see how she's doing. That bothers her—along with all the other things. In fact, the list could go on and on.

Whether you are a woman or a man, if you find yourself identifying with any of Jane's experiences and concerns, this book is for you.

Many people these days have some understanding that their childhoods were less than what they should have been—or outright abusive. They have learned what abuse really is, felt some pain, sadness, and anger. As they have also learned that their parents were probably no better off as children than they were, they have made efforts to forgive. Yet their lives are still not going very well.

Some have come to this awareness only recently; perhaps this is the first such book they have picked up. Others have known for years. Regardless of when your interest in understanding how your childhood influenced you began, regardless of how much you have already done to try to understand it, if you still find yourself hungrily browsing bookstore aisles for new titles or new information, this book is for you.

This book will provide you with an understanding of "regressive" methods you can use to enable yourself to heal from the effects of having spent your childhood in a family that was not able to give you what you needed to thrive. It will discuss what those methods are, why they are needed, and how they work. It will offer examples of the ways in which our childhoods continue to affect our daily interactions with people. Perhaps most important, it will present detailed steps that can be used by anyone to further his or her own growth.

BEGINNING AT THE BEGINNING

The first thing to understand in beginning this work is that *there are experiences that are too painful for children to feel. There are also certain realities, certain truths about our parents and our families, that are too painful for children to know about.* Children, who are powerless to change these situations, come to rely on the self-protective defenses of *repression*—forcing the memory of the event into the unconscious mind—and *denial*—refusing to acknowledge the truth before them.

The extent to which a parent's uncaring behaviors and personal limitations can hurt a child is grossly underestimated in our culture, even among those with enough understanding to recognize themselves as "adult children." ·

The writer who most successfully addresses this miscalculation is Swiss author Alice Miller, who resigned from her practice as a Freudian psychoanalyst in order to inform the world of the routinely abusive nature of Western child-rearing practices. Miller, who has no affiliation with the recovery movement in North America, addresses the problem at its childhood core and focuses treatment at this source, something current writers of popular therapeutic literature do not usually do. Portions of Dr. Miller's first book, *Prisoners of Childhood: The Drama of the Gifted Child and the Search for the True Self,* were originally papers written in 1979 for publication in professional psychoanalytic journals. These papers brought her much recognition. It was only in 1981, after she described her discovery of the frequency of sexual child abuse and Freud's suppression of this truth in *Thou Shalt Not Be Aware,* that her colleagues reacted with hostility. This brought her face to face with tremendous denial, even among professionals, of the fact that the lives of children in comfortable, industrialized Western society are in reality full of painful experiences. This realization caused her to sever her affil-

iation with the International Psychoanalytic Association and devote
herself to further writing on the subject.

It is clear to me that the resistance Alice Miller encountered
more than a decade ago is alive and well today, especially among
professionals (see Miller's *Breaking Down the Walls of Silence*)—in
spite of the information available about child abuse and the recognition that the term encompasses more than physical or sexual as-
sault. Still minimized and ignored is the *extent* to which *any* abuse
hurts a small child.

A NATION IN DENIAL

The reason for this societywide minimization is that we are a nation
"in denial." The fact that physical and sexual abuse does occur,
more often than anyone could imagine, has recently become a popular theme. That adults are able, through psychotherapy, to recall
formerly repressed events has been validated by the acceptance of
such memories as evidence sufficient to trigger investigations into
unsolved crimes, or as a basis for adults to sue their parents, regardless of the number of intervening years during which the memory
was not conscious. These situations have also been the basis for
television and movie dramatizations.

Despite this public dissemination of information—about the
facts that children are currently being abused by their families and
that the children of an earlier generation, now adults, continue to
suffer the effects of those experiences and need to seek therapy—
the general public still seems to be ignorant of the lasting effects
of such abusive treatment. Worse, accused parents and their sup-
porters have counterattacked, accusing their children of false memory syndrome (FMS) and claiming that they had been hypnotized
or otherwise influenced by therapists to believe such things. In the
interest of "fairness," these counterattacks are given great attention, and are cited by some as persuasive evidence that the abuse
did not take place. Even some of the "children" claim they
came to find out that their "memories" were false. One is tempted

to ask, "How?" Because the parents assure them that the abuse didn't happen?

Unfortunately, though, even if society can no longer reasonably deny that this abuse happens, the desire to cling to the idea that abusive experiences in childhood have little or no serious effect on the adults these children become is still strong. Society denies this reality because almost everyone has been the recipient of some abuse in childhood (emotional, if not physical or sexual). Thus the protective mechanism of "repression" has been called into play by almost everyone at some point while growing up. Admitting the reality of widespread childhood abuse is a threat to each individual's denial of family experiences, so only those ready to face them—those whose memories have already begun to surface, or who have been experiencing disturbing but disconnected symptoms—are likely to be open to this information.

Repression causes any reality or event that is too painful to deal with to be blocked from conscious awareness, totally or in part—enough to allow the child to continue life as if the event were not true, had not happened, or was not important. Then, as the child matures, denial enables him or her to continue to operate "as if."

The unconscious defenses of repression and denial work together to protect human beings from the awareness of truths or experiences that could threaten their survival.

TRAUMA AND REPRESSION

It is not just in childhood that these mechanisms are utilized. Any traumatic experience, at any age, may be repressed to the extent that the individual never remembers it consciously. Despite repression, however, pieces of the memory eventually break through for some people, as in the case of the "flashbacks" that troubled those veterans of the war in Vietnam whose experiences were too painful to process. Many of those whose memories broke through the repressive system sought treatment, as they found themselves overwhelmed by feelings and mental anguish that had been blocked by their unconscious to prevent them from breaking down while in combat. Posttraumatic stress disorder (PTSD), as this condition has come to be called, has generally been understood to be something that affects adults who undergo traumas causing extreme distress that is blocked from consciousness and is not initially recognized for what it is when it surfaces later.

Adults working in therapy to access repressed childhood memories find the process to be very frightening and painful. As memories surface, the emotions that were buried with childhood experiences feel as overwhelming as those described by Vietnam veterans.

A logical deduction can be made that the phenomenon of the adult child or co-dependent is in essence the same as that of the Vietnam veteran suffering from posttraumatic stress disorder. Some writers have recognized this connection and have suggested that co-dependency be diagnosed as PTSD. Entertaining such a comparison, however, means accepting the idea that people's childhoods can and do contain horrors comparable to combat, the effects of which call for intensive treatment rather than merely learning new, "corrective" behaviors. Not surprisingly, then, this notion has not gained great acceptance because our cultural denial rejects both the idea that we adults have all experienced such severe trauma and the idea that our children, in turn, are living through assaults on their psyches as damaging as those sustained by soldiers in battle.

Only those courageous people who have allowed themselves to regress fully into blocked childhood experiences truly know how painful the events in question really were. The pain involved is beyond the imagination of the uninitiated person; indeed, it takes an act of faith, even for those "in recovery," to accept the idea that such painful events may have taken place. It is extremely important, however, that this possibility be accepted as a working hypothesis, to be proved or disproved as one explores what is waiting behind the repressive blocks in one's own, very personal history.

THE PRICE OF REPRESSION

It is common to think of "normal" people—those whose repressive systems block memories of childhood abuse so totally that they are never affected in any obvious way—as better off than those who seek therapy. It's the old idea that "what you don't know can't hurt you." And superficially, perhaps their lives do seem easier—but this ease comes at great cost. Even though the individual may be unaware of it, a high price is paid by anyone in such total denial and those with whom he or she has relationships, particularly children. Life cannot be emotionally full and rich, because the unconscious is continually sorting out and rejecting or altering any stimulus that might threaten to arouse unwanted memories.

Sheryl, for instance, has always unconsciously avoided living in houses with second stories, so she would never have to hear someone coming up the stairs in the night. Unbeknownst to Sheryl, there was a buried memory connected to that sound. The sound itself is innocent, but the memory of which it is a part is not. Sheryl might remember the experience in its entirety someday if she were subject to a re-creation of only the beginning part. Her avoidance of houses with second stories, apparently so benign, helps ensure that the repressive block remains in place.

Any kind of external stimulus can carry this type of threat. For example, Stephen is not comfortable living on a noisy street, while Joanne can't stand it if it's "too quiet." Alissa will not have anything but modern furniture and is anxious when visiting her out-of-town friends who are antique lovers. She never sleeps well in their house and doesn't understand why. Anita has to make sure bedroom doors are fully opened or closed, since the light from a crack in the partly opened door of a dark room at night frightens her. Patrick hates the muffled sound of a television through the wall; Ben can't abide household disorder; Tina will not eat in restaurants where people can't sit with their backs to the wall or work in an office with spaces created by modular units instead of wall-to-ceiling partitions. Gloria avoids movie theaters and other close, crowded places because of an aversion to other people's "annoying" habits such as knuckle cracking and gum chewing.

These behaviors of avoidance are not usually obvious to an outside observer but, should someone pose a question regarding them, they would be given some rational explanation. The conscious mind provides an excuse for others as well as for the person himself (who is often aware of the motivating fear without knowing its source). "I hate having to always run upstairs to get something," Sheryl might say about her choice of houses, while Alissa might say, "I've never liked that furniture." "I get chilly (or too hot) eating on patios," Ben might say, or "I don't like their food." Similarly, one can simply find virtue in having a perfectly clean house (or comfort in a messy one), or find another reason to choose a job that is in a building with closed offices. One can find other explanations for always being the last one in the household to go to bed, or using night lights in every room plus the hall, and so forth. Except in extreme cases, which are often labeled "phobias," this sorting out is done so smoothly that it simply becomes part of the person's "personality" and is never seen as anything more than that.

When the threatening stimulus is a salient characteristic of someone with whom a totally repressed person has an intimate relationship, this sorting and altering then extends to the other person's way of being. This means that some part of a partner or spouse cannot be expressed or accepted. For instance, someone who tends to wonder about things may be inclined to question a companion about her or his ideas, not expecting the other person to really know any answers, but if this touches on some unconscious and painful childhood reality, such as unrealistic expectations to perform, the questioner will be responded to defensively in some way. Any personal habit, such as putting one's fingers to one's mouth when concentrating on a problem, can arouse similar defensiveness. If characteristics such as laughing loudly, telling jokes at parties, or being passive in social situations—anything, really—happen to match characteristics of an abusive adult from childhood, trouble will arise in the relationship over these behaviors. The result can be an attitude of constant criticism on the part of the repressed person—which may be expressed directly ("Stop scratching your head all the time!") or indirectly (with exasperated sighs, eye rolling, and the like). When this situation is found in marriage or other close life partnerships, both people tend to be unhappy, with one feeling angry and the other victimized. Overt fighting over inconsequential things may become a near-daily event, or an undercurrent of subtle, indirect, passive-aggressive hostility may be present. It is not uncommon that one member of a couple like this will belittle or tear down the other when they are socializing.

Most children of such people unconsciously change themselves in hope of finding approval and/or avoiding abuse. Each then becomes what Alice Miller, in *The Drama of the Gifted Child*, calls a "false self," and continues to perpetuate the problem down through following generations.

REPRESSION AND DISTORTED REALITY

Another serious consequence of continued repression has to do with the way in which the unconscious is forced to function in order to maintain it. The sorting-out requires that reality be distorted sufficiently to control the impact of any particular event. In other words, an inborn human capacity—the ability to process experience—is damaged.

In order to process experience fully and realistically, a person must first be able to see clearly what is happening in a given situation. This sounds both obvious and simple, as if it were always the case. When a high level of denial is present, however, clear perceptions are more the exception than the rule. Instead, what usually happens is that the unconscious distorts perceptions without the individual's being aware of it.

This hampers the individual's capacity adequately to perform the next step in processing: to explain the event rationally, to make mental sense out of it. Such explanations are reasonably accurate if perceptions are undistorted; denial, however, results in faulty explanations, so that events are frequently misunderstood and either too little or too much is read into them. The unconscious, acting on the basis of unfelt childhood abuse and the denial that protects the mind from becoming aware of it, can cause an individual either to decide that something is true that isn't, or decide that something isn't true that is.

The ability to be aware of any emotional response aroused by the event is also a necessary part of processing an experience, but it is very rare that the individual can do this. Either emotions are totally shut down, so that nothing is felt, or an overreaction occurs. In either case, most people do not really know what they feel. Often, an ordinary event that causes a strong emotional response (whether or not the person is aware of this response) has an unconscious connection to an earlier, painful event from childhood that has been repressed. The experience in the present "triggers" the memory of the past event, so that an overly strong reaction, or lack of any reaction at all, instead of a normal feeling, results. When this happens, a relatively minor lapse such as forgetting a dentist appointment may cause panic, while something more important, such as discovering that the IRS is auditing a tax return on which you have failed to disclose all your income, may be shrugged off as if it were nothing.

PROCESSING EXPERIENCE

The purpose of repression is to protect our survival—and it works. We did grow up into adulthood. However, as we have seen, repression damages a very important human capacity: the ability to process experience, which is essential to a sane, satisfying life. The five necessary steps in this process are:

1. To perceive external reality accurately—that is, when something happens, you know what happened.
2. To make rational sense of that reality—to use your conscious mind to think about what happened and come to some reasonably accurate understanding of it.

3. To accurately perceive one's own emotional reactions to that reality—to know how an event makes you feel.
4. To determine viable response options while considering external reality—to decide what you want to do in response and estimate the probable consequences.
5. To choose an option based on your own best interest, or the best interest of a child or other dependent.

REPRESSION AND DENIAL IN ACTION

When the life-saving repressive process interferes with this natural ability to process experience, we almost always mishandle the difficult events that periodically occur in our lives. Let's look at two specific cases.

Bob has a dog and Jack, his new neighbor, doesn't. One morning Bob finds that Jack has driven his car across his front lawn, leaving ruts and tread marks on the grass. Bob figures his neighbor didn't realize what he was doing and decides just to let it go, so as not to cause problems. Several days later Bob realizes that Jack has continued to drive his car across the front of his lawn when returning home. Bob's wife wants him to go next door and say something, but he tells her that Jack must somehow need the space for parking; the lawn is full of dandelions anyway, so who cares? Much later, Jack's wife tells Bob's wife that her husband is angry because their dog continually relieves itself on Jack's lawn. Recurrent, damaging action on the part of his neighbor probably should have made Bob angry, but his unconscious, afraid of confrontation, provided an explanation of Jack's behavior that would allow Bob to bypass legitimate anger.

In another version of this scenario, when Jenna first sees that her neighbor, Jules, has driven across the front of her lawn, she wonders if Jules is angry at her for something she did. She is stricken with fear, and that night she has a dream in which someone is chasing her with a knife. She awakes in terror, drenched with sweat. When Jenna's friend, Doreen, calls the next day to catch up, Jenna tells her about her dream and about her worry that she has somehow offended Jules. She's afraid of the guy and can talk about nothing else.

Doreen tells Jenna to calm down, since there may be an explanation that has nothing to do with anything she has done and she may be taking it too personally. The next day Jules's wife tells Jenna that Jules had come home drunk on the night in question and felt terrible when he saw what he had done. She expected he would soon talk to Jenna about paying for the damage.

As we have seen, Bob's explanation of his neighbor's behavior resulted in no overt emotional reaction at all; instead, it allowed for complete denial of a need to feel anything about it. In Jenna's case, the emotional overreaction of fear accompanied the explanation. Neither reaction was appropriate to the situation at hand, but both reactions were appropriate to the childhood histories of these two people.

Bob had a mother who was emotionally fragile and took to her bed for days if any altercation occurred in the family; both parents blamed the children for "upsetting Mother." Bob and his brothers and sisters were not only deprived of their mother's presence and the nurturing they should have received from her, but they were made to feel guilty as well. Coming from such a childhood, it is natural for Bob, as an adult, to try to avoid causing any "upset," no matter what is done to him. It is also natural that Bob has no conscious understanding of *why* this happens, as the original trauma of his mother's absences and the accompanying guilt has long since been repressed.

Jenna, on the other hand, had a hostile and capricious father who found fault with any little thing she did. When her father was upset with her, he would hit her with a belt. Because her father's anger was unpredictable, Jenna could never figure out what to do or avoid doing to be safe. Since she was a child, Jenna was a helpless victim, powerless to stop this mistreatment. Jenna was fearful all the time, but could not consciously remember this as an adult since the memory was repressed. Now this repressed fear emerges whenever it appears that someone is angry at her. Because of her father's relentless abuse, Jenna unconsciously expects that any act resembling an attack is caused by anger at her for something she has done even though it certainly is not clear to her that she has actually done anything to provoke the anger. Intense fear threatens to overwhelm her, but instead emerges in dreams, in obsessive rumination about the incident, or in general "worry." She is unaware of the source of this, and believes she has good cause for it now.

In cases such as Bob's and Jenna's, there is very little chance that the final step in processing an experience—determining an effective, realistic response—will happen, since the information upon which the response must be based has been distorted by the unconscious. If Bob's and Jack's wives had not communicated with each other, the situation no doubt would have been mishandled. In Bob's situation, there certainly would have been conflict between Bob and his wife, since he wanted to ignore it; or Bob's wife might have taken the matter into her own hands and angrily confronted their neighbors, inciting further bad feelings. In Jenna's situation, it's likely that her anxiety would have quietly continued until Jules related to her in an obviously friendly way, took responsibility for the incident in a manner that clearly showed there was no malice attached to it, or, as actually happened, Jules's wife explained what really happened and why.

When painful childhood experiences are repressed, people either miss completely or misunderstand much of what happens to them, and often engage in responses that are totally inappropriate to the present event. It appears that what we don't know *can* hurt us—a lot!

UNDERREACTION AND OVERREACTION

Bob's underreaction and Jenna's overreaction indicate that the defenses of repression and denial unconsciously implemented by a child for protection can result in two seemingly very different forms of adult behavior.

Underreaction comes from emotional "shutdown," while overreaction comes from an ability to feel the emotion—Jenna can certainly feel her intense fear—but the emotion is connected to her childhood, not the present incident. Most people can recognize the tendency toward one or the other response among their friends and spouses or in themselves. Some of us are usually outgoing, talkative, and "over"-emotional, while others are more often quiet, solitary, and emotionally closed. Most people respond to situations predominantly one way or the other, but experience shows that far more men than women are seen as shut down and far more women than men could be called overemotional. Regardless, none of us, men or women, always react either way. We all do both, depending on the situation. However, for our purposes I would like to refer to the group of men as (mostly) "underreactive," and to their female counterparts as (mostly) "overreactive." This is an oversimplification, which can be discarded later when we explore the details of the repressive process and how these two responses originate, but it will do for now.

It is usually people who tend to overreact who want to work to undo the effects of their family histories—if they can see the connection between their childhoods and their present problems, and if their situations are not masked because of substance abuse or other addictive behaviors. Those people who more often underreact to stimuli are less driven to seek help, as they are disconnected from most of their potentially uncomfortable feelings. They may have relationship problems, or be pressed by those close to them to "open up more," but they often see this as the other person's problem. Before more than a small minority of our population will be motivated to face their pasts, however, it must be recognized that almost all the adults in our society have been affected and that our child-rearing practices *at their best* make the proverbial "happy childhood" a myth.

THE ROLE OF GRIEF IN HEALING

People often wonder why they need to "dredge all that up" in order to heal. To many, delving into the past seems to invite suffering that can do no good, since it was "all so long ago." People think this way because they don't know about a healing process we are all

born with, which goes largely unappreciated and undeveloped because of our parents' ignorance. This process is sanctioned later in
life only in one particular circumstance—in the aftermath of a loved
one's death. That process is grief.

Grief has only recently been given the attention it deserves,
even as the way people are able to deal with the painful loss of a
loved one. It was not so long ago that the suppression of *any* emotional suffering was admired: the "stiff upper lip" was considered
a sign of "self-command" and "good breeding." Since women
were considered the "weaker" sex, they were allowed to weep (as
long as they didn't "overdo it"), but "strong" men were never supposed to cry. (Obviously, this cultural attitude has a direct bearing
on why the under- and overreactive phenomenon divides primarily
along gender lines.) Fortunately, many men have become aware
that this cultural conditioning has cheated them out of a valuable
way to handle the pain of loss, and they have reclaimed their tears.

Grief, however, should not be seen only as something appropriate in regard to loss through death. Any loss—and anything that
causes emotional pain *is* a loss—can be healed by grieving it. In
order to be able to grieve, though, people need first to admit the
loss, but, as is generally known, denial of loss is so common that
it is actually considered an initial step in the grieving process!
Once the denial no longer works, and the loss has to be acknowledged, anger steps in as a secondary defense against the pain.
This, too, is so common it is described as part of the process of
grieving in Elisabeth Kübler-Ross's landmark work, *On Death and
Dying*.

It is difficult to grieve in our culture. People have learned to
defend themselves automatically against emotional pain. In addition, the need to grieve, to feel the pain, is considered acceptable
only under very specific circumstances—when someone dies.
Even then, there is a strong notion that people can grieve "too
long," that at a certain point they need to "get on with their lives."
All of this curtailment exists because people do not really understand what grief is or how to use it to heal. Such understanding
cannot occur until we admit how much we are hurt by certain

kinds of treatment from others, especially mistreatment in childhood from our parents or other caregivers. As long as people deny this truth, the grief process will continue to be seen as unnecessary, expressing emotional pain at all will be seen as useless, perhaps even unhealthy, and the key to truly resolving painful experiences in our lives will go unused.

chapter two

Abuse, Repression, and Childhood Consciousness

Repression first arises during childhood in response to the abuse most children undergo because their parents are unable to give them what they need. Parental incapacity ranges in degree from simple emotional ignorance, inadequacy, or unavailability to extremely dangerous and insane mistreatment. The latter is easily accepted as abusive by most people, but less readily received is the idea that, unless worked through therapeutically, *abuse always results in lifelong affliction.*

For our purposes, we need to allow not only that childhood abuse affects us all our lives, but that behavior as "harmless" as an angry look, a yell, a smack on the bottom, an impatiently yanked arm, disapproval of normal childhood activity and personality traits, and the demand for perfection is in fact abusive. I do not mean to imply that parents will ruin their children if they are not perfect. All mothers and fathers will respond in some of these ways to their children—it is impossible not to. But parents *can* recognize that these behaviors are not appropriate responses to their children and

take steps that will help their children process an experience instead
of repressing it.

RECOGNIZING ABUSE

When adults, especially mothers, start realizing that certain traditional ways of handling children are actually abusive, they begin to
worry about the harm they may have inadvertently done to their
own children. This is natural, and it is important to begin to make
changes based on this new understanding—but their first priority
must be to become aware of whatever it was they experienced as
abusive in their own childhood families. As they recover from unresolved pain and loss, they will automatically become more nurturing toward their own children, since then their hearts will naturally
tell them what is right. The less repression protects them from the
pain of their own childhoods, the less possible it is for them to behave in ways that will hurt their children. It is being disconnected
from their own pain that allows parents to be abusive without knowing it. Once this connection is restored, they can feel the pain of
their children and know what hurts them. Since perfection is impossible, they will not always *do* what is right, but their awareness that
something wrong has happened will enable them to handle the mis-
step in a loving way for the child so the effects can be processed.
The child's unconscious does not have to block what happened or
how much it hurt, since the parent is present to help the child acknowledge the pain as it arises.

How might this look? After Phil had had a bad day at work,
Richard, his eleven-year-old son, was talking about what had happened at school that day. "Dad," he said, "the teacher said that if we
keep on allowing stream erosion and don't stop polluting our rivers,
pretty soon we won't have any drinkable water." Phil was in no
mood to discuss environmental issues, and angrily retorted, "Your
teacher is probably one of those people who know nothing about
science and how it can be used to solve problems like that. You are
stupid to listen to her. I told you before you have to learn to think
for yourself, not believe everything you're told." Richard became

flustered and burst into tears, only to hear his father yell, "Go to your room. If you can't sit here and have a discussion without crying, you don't belong at the dinner table!" But Phil soon realized how unkind and unfair he had been. He went to Richard, who was still crying, hugged him, apologized, and explained that his day at work had left him in a foul mood and he had unfairly taken it out on Richard. Phil also listened while Richard told him how bad it made him feel—that it hurt and made him angry. He accepted his son's feelings, telling him he would have felt that way, too. Then they returned together to the dinner table.

In such an environment, repression is not necessary, so the child's ability to process experience remains intact. This is the kind of healthy family interaction that is possible for those who are willing to face the repressed pain of their own childhoods.

THE USE OF REPRESSION

As research continues, it becomes more and more evident that children are intelligent beings, from the very first, and that infants are far more developed, both emotionally and mentally, than was previously thought.

Children have enough understanding to recognize when they are being mistreated; but if they were to allow that understanding, the next logical step would be to sense that the love they need to thrive is missing. When put together, these two things—the conscious knowledge that the people on whom they depend for their very lives are mistreating them, and the awareness that they are not loved as they need to be—constitute a survival threat to the child's psyche. The experience is akin to being a prisoner of war or an inmate in a concentration camp, since the well-being of the dependent individual is not a priority to those with the power.

Adults who have survived such wartime experiences report that, in order to protect themselves from the feeling of helplessness generated by being at the mercy of hostile, uncaring people, they had to find a way to take themselves out of that reality mentally. Years ago I read an article that described how a prisoner of war mentally built a house, board by board, to keep the horrible truth of his situation at bay. The plan was so detailed that, after the man was rescued, he was able to follow his mental plan and actually construct a house from it.

This is one example of the defensive maneuvers that people use to avoid feeling the full impact of a painful situation in which one is helpless to effect change. Like the Vietnam-era soldiers who repressed their experiences, this prisoner also found a way to "escape" his situation. However, this method was used consciously, unlike repression, a process that takes place without the individual's awareness.

For adults, the mind's survival maneuvers can be either unconscious or conscious. When the underlying premise of the situation is acceptable (in war, we *expect* the enemy to be uninterested in our welfare), the trauma stems entirely from the treatment we receive, not from a *meaning* we cannot allow ourselves to admit. This allows us to deal with it on a conscious level. In childhood, however, our parents are precisely the people we must believe to be most interested in our welfare as a top priority. Any realization that this might be untrue is untenable (just as the order to massacre women and children in Vietnam was untenable to the soldiers). When the trauma involves facing an emotional reality we cannot handle, the "escape" has to be unconscious.

From reading or hearing about such accounts, most people are aware that our minds protect us in these ways. But few know why. The reason is that human beings are able to survive horrible events, as long as they can avoid feeling hopeless. Simply put, hope keeps people alive. The opposite is also true: hopelessness can kill. One way to stay alive is to escape consciously by keeping the mind busy with something else. Another is to repress the reality, using denial as an aid.

THE USE OF DENIAL

The comparison drawn between these wartime adult experiences and childhood does not so much address the idea that our children are being treated badly as it does the helpless dependence of small children, which places them in as vulnerable a position in relation to their parent(s) as prisoners are in relation to their captors. This powerless vulnerability is what can lead to a feeling of hopelessness so strong it can kill. If admitted, the full reality of certain terrible situations can threaten the life of an adult; it is even more dangerous for a child because the organism, not being fully developed, is so vulnerable. Denial protects the child from being overwhelmed by this feeling, thereby protecting its life.

Many children use denial in this way to allow them to maintain an unconscious sense of hope. They thus construct a "false self"—a self that will be driven to try to be whatever their unconscious thinks will bring them love. This is usually an attempt to please the unloving parent enough to make that parent change into what the child needs. It is sometimes called "false" or "unreal" hope because it is a substitute for what is always a hopeless reality. For example, if a child has an overworked and stressed mother, he may tell himself that, if he can help Mom enough (even though he is not old enough to be a real help), she will become available to him. Or he may tell himself that if he can be outstanding in some way, such as getting good grades at school, becoming a star athlete or an admired dramatic performer at school, then she will have to notice how special he is and pay more attention to him.

Another type of denial is to believe that whatever is happening is not important—that it doesn't hurt you, doesn't matter, or is somehow "good for you." When this defense is used, the individual becomes disconnected from his feelings. Not being able to *feel* is a sure way to be able to believe that something isn't emotionally disturbing.

Each of these defenses is something of which the child is unaware and serves as an effective protection against the hopelessness that has the power to kill.

THE REALITY OF ABUSE

Although most families do not inhumanly abuse their children, I would encourage you to consider that a parent's unavailability, disapproval, or preoccupation are forms of neglect that subject the child to an experience far worse than you might have reason to anticipate. Small children are totally dependent upon the nurture and caring of their parents. They need much more than food, clothing, shelter, and dry diapers: they need to feel loved, they need to be held, softly talked to, laughed with, cradled in someone's arms, sung to sleep. They need to sense that the arms around them are happy to hold their little body; that the bath they get is a pleasure to give; that the voice that sings their bedtime lullaby has no strain in it from a recent argument; that their very presence in their father's and mother's lives is a joy.

Again, while we as parents cannot provide these things perfectly, they are nevertheless what our children need—and the extent to which they are not provided causes the children pain. The less capable the parents, the worse the pain and the greater the probability that the child is in danger of feeling as uncared about and hopeless as a prisoner of war. For this reason, small children cannot let themselves be aware that their caregivers are incapable (possibly to the point of being dangerous) without jeopardizing their own survival. To protect against this risk, the mind automatically steps in with the power of the unconscious to block these facts and their meanings. As we have seen, this blocking is called repression. Since its function is to prevent awareness, once repression is in place children will not fully comprehend what is happening to them and why.

OVER- AND UNDERREACTION

Children who develop false hope may believe that mistreatment is justified, that they deserve it because they are not "good enough." Such children, most often female, will grow into adults with low self-esteem who cannot set limits with—or even recognize mistreatment from—peers and who keep trying to be "better." Attempts to change by learning how to set limits or by engaging in self-esteem exercises will be largely ineffective, until the original block to what couldn't be known and felt in childhood is removed, so that the original pain can be known and felt.

Some other children, usually male, deaden themselves to any feelings at all in order to believe that they cannot be hurt by what their parents do. They grow into underreactive adults who cannot relate with true intimacy to the people most important to them. Getting in touch with their "maleness," beating drums, or even allowing themselves to yell with anger and cry with despair can be a beginning—but unless the original experiences that required them to become dead emotionally are faced, there will be no substantial healing.

It is natural to speculate about why more men than women are found among the underreactors while the opposite can be observed about women. Our patriarchal culture certainly encourages males to suppress feelings, to be "strong" and "in control." Little boys are routinely ridiculed for showing tender feelings, the ridicule often taking the form of derision at being "like a girl." At the same time, aggression is encouraged, as well as heroism. These messages are absorbed, and the fastest way to attempt to fulfill society's expectations is simply to repress any of the feelings found unacceptable.

Not long ago I overheard a discussion between two men who had recently become fathers. Both belonged to the group of men who are striving to be more emotionally open and certainly would be considered "feminists." Both had been present at the circumcisions of their male babies, and they were attempting to talk about how they felt about witnessing this event, which was so obviously painful for their sons. Each of them kept using the word *intense* over and over. "Yeah, it was really intense." "Boy, was it ever intense." Although the word was not enough, they kept trying to find relief in verbal sharing—but the necessary words were not part of their vocabulary.

Women in this situation could have talked about how much it hurt them to see their child's pain, because, as little girls they are not told to be tough and strong or to express only a narrow range of emotions, as are little boys. On the other hand, little girls are discouraged from expressing aggressiveness and a desire for power. "Weak" emotions, like sadness, loss, and helplessness, are allowed, approved of, and can bring comfort. If females are culturally allowed to feel emotional pain (weakness) but not anger (strength), and the opposite is so for males, it would be logical that women would tend to overreact and men to underreact when faced with emotionally charged situations.

THE ROLE OF THE UNCONSCIOUS

Almost all of us come from families in which we experienced abuse of some kind. For many, the abuse was either ongoing or severe enough that, at some crucial point, both the experiences and their meaning were repressed. This resulted in our becoming unaware on a conscious level of the full reality of what was happening to us. Since the process was unconscious, we didn't realize it had taken place.

The mechanism of repression ensured our survival. We grew up into adulthood. But because our ability to process experiences was damaged, repression (which enabled us to get through an abusive childhood in as much comfort as possible—or, in some cases, enabled us to get through it at all) becomes a liability for the adult. The unconscious continues to protect us from something from which we no longer need protection—the full awareness of what happened and the accompanying painful feelings.

Since repression and denial stem from the unconscious part of our minds, they continue to operate automatically; we are not consciously aware of their activity because the conscious and unconscious parts of our minds have different functions and capacities. It is the conscious part that distinguishes between the present and the past (we are consciously aware of our age, living circumstances, abilities as adults, etc.), while the unconscious part does not understand anything about time—yet is capable of altering the conscious mind's reality perceptions. Thus the protective mechanisms we needed as children still function despite the fact that we no longer need them.

They function so well, in fact, that the feelings of fear, sadness, loss, shame, anger, and hopelessness, to name a few, from which we were protected as children are either totally shut off from our awareness so that we are unable to feel them at all or, when we do feel them now, they appear to be caused by events in our present lives. In response, we either under- or overreact. The inability to feel these painful feelings at all, or the tendency to feel them but attach them to present reality, interferes with our present capacity to process experiences accurately. This causes no end of difficulties, particularly in relationships. Unfortunately, most popular methods of treatment do not address this unconscious influence.

THE STATE OF CHILDHOOD CONSCIOUSNESS

The memories that are buried—both what happened (or what was true) and the pain connected to what happened—are retained in *childhood form.* And the degree of consciousness a child has is different from that of an adult: things don't look the same to children as they do to adults. The world of a child is very limited, until at least junior high school age. Your parents and/or siblings, and the way things are done in your family, seem like standards. You accept as fact the belief that your parents are right about things, and that everyone lives in a family like yours. Due to youth and inexperience, you have no perspective, no objective standards. If your mother scowls at you for doing something appropriate for your age, like exploring the contents of a purse that she left where you could reach it, you feel like a bad child. The bad feeling (shame) is very painful.

In the childhood state of consciousness, the relativity of things is unknown. The capacity to realize that Mother's disapproval will not last forever has not yet developed; there is no recognition that things begin and end, that time changes things, or that even though she disapproves, you may not in fact be doing anything wrong. Her scowl, then, has a very powerful effect, and you may begin to fear that Mother doesn't like you and never will, or, even worse, that you are not worth liking. Also, when something painful happens in early childhood—a smashed toy, for instance—a child feels as if his life is wrecked; he may weep as if his heart is broken in such a situation. Here again, the child has no awareness that, although the loss hurts, it is relatively unimportant in the greater scheme of things.

In addition, children have fears that seem, to an adult, to be totally without cause. For instance, when my daughter was four years old, she was afraid of taking baths because she thought an alligator might get into the tub. Even when we didn't use bubble bath, so that she could see through to the bottom of the tub, she was afraid. When I asked her how she thought an alligator—a rather big creature, after all—could get into the bathtub, she said, in a quavering voice, "Through the faucet?"

Childhood feelings are powerful in the best of circumstances. Small losses are devastating, and unwarranted fears are very real. The fact that children are dependent beings in a situation where they inherently have little or no power—usually in families where the parents are incapable of meeting all their needs—adds to the emotional impact of events that, from the adult point of view, seem harmless. The childhood state of consciousness, then, is one in which both the thinking and the feeling processes are *qualitatively different* from what they will be in the adult state.

As we can see, focusing on changing unproductive adult behaviors is not going to get to the root of the problem. That root is beneath the unconscious block that stands between us and awareness of old childhood abuse experiences. Both the "fact" of the events (what actually happened, who was there, what was said, who did what, where you were, how old you were) and the "feelings" (the full emotional impact of what happened) are hidden behind that block. Often these memories are not *completely* absent from our conscious awareness, but we are missing either the fact or the feeling, or we have used denial to change the meaning so as to avoid its full impact.

HEALING AND THE CHILDHOOD CONSCIOUSNESS

For healing to take place, this unconscious block must be removed so the original event and its pain can be processed. This does *not* mean trying to remember childhood, talking about it, or crying about it. These activities are engaged in by the conscious mind— and not only the conscious mind, but the *adult* conscious mind. In other words, when we try to remember childhood in order to talk or cry about it, we are doing so *from our adult state of consciousness.* Yet this is what people are often advised to do, under the misnomer of "grief work." There is a serious mistake here, for *the feelings that need to be processed happened in childhood, and therefore continue to exist in the childhood state of consciousness.* It is the grief of this child, the child we were, that we need to feel.

This childhood state of consciousness—and the child's grief caused by the abuse experienced in childhood—resides in the unconscious, along with all or some of the memories, blocked by repression. It is *in this state* that we must face the reality of that abuse and feel the pain, for it was *then* that the experiences were not processed. The miracle of the mind is that the unconscious holds the experiences in the exact forms in which they happened. They can be retrieved, and processed, any time in the future, no matter how old we become. But to do so we have to realize what that state is, how we feel when we are in it, and what to do with it. When these things are understood, we are able to fully know what happened and to be in the grief of the child we were—a desirable place to be, for that is the grief that heals.

chapter three

Childhood
Consciousness Versus
Adult Reality

All adults return to the childhood state of consciousness with some frequency, although they are unaware of it. Whenever we under- or overreact to something, the mind has shifted from the adult state of consciousness to that of childhood, and we temporarily experience the world from the dependent position of the child. Either we are flooded with feelings that are out of proportion to present reality, or we shut down emotionally, automatically defending ourselves from a potential onslaught. In the latter situation, we are not even aware that feelings are present, waiting to be felt.

SHIFTING INTO THE CHILDHOOD STATE

Let's look at a typical situation in which an adult suddenly "becomes a child" emotionally. One winter morning, Joan walks outside to get into her car to go to work. The previous evening she had parked the car outside the garage, and this morning she finds that a heavy load of melting snow with layers of ice has slid off the metal roof of the garage onto the windshield, crushing it completely. Feeling overwhelmed and berating herself for her "stupidity" in parking the car there, Joan bursts into tears. Crying, she rushes back inside, interrupting her husband, George, who is shaving, to tell him what has happened and how stupid she has been. George puts down his razor, gives her a hug, and tells her that she couldn't have known this would happen and that she shouldn't blame herself. Still sobbing, Joan then says that she doesn't know how she'll get to work or what to do about the car. George suggests she call coworkers who live nearby, or, if worse comes to worst, they will both go in his car and one of them will just be late for work. Once at work, Joan can call her insurance company for directions on where and how to get the car fixed. Joan is now able to dry her tears and follow George's suggestions. She finally begins to feel "like herself" again while she is talking to the insurance agent.

The telltale signs of Joan's shift into a childhood state of consciousness were the rush of emotion that overwhelmed her and her intense need to "run to" someone to be reassured and told what to do. Looking to someone else to "be the adult" for us is a sure sign that we have lost our adult perspective on experience and have become "children." It is often not until later that people can recognize that their emotional response was out of proportion to the incident.

As we have seen, none of the solutions George offered was anything that Joan could not have thought of for herself. When she is functioning as an adult, Joan can call upon her intelligence and experience with life to know what to do. The suddenness and severity of the situation, however, caused a mind shift that sent her back to a state where she had a child's limited experience and knowledge of the world; in this childhood state, the appropriate responses were temporarily unavailable to her. We can deduce that Joan's family was one in which blame was assessed when things went wrong, since she also felt shame and called herself "stupid," thereby adding insult to injury. She ran to her husband (who, to her unconscious, became her parent) for the adult capabilities she temporarily lacked. She also ran to him in hope she would be comforted, not blamed. In this case, George was able to provide her with the caring Joan felt she needed.

It is important to note that Joan's shift back into her present, adult state of feeling and thinking happened automatically, and did not depend on George's response. Further, George's response was positive; in many cases, the person is not so fortunate. Had George been preparing for an important appointment, he may well have been impatient and angry at Joan for needing him to do what "should have been obvious" to her. Given this circumstance, he might also have blamed her for "being so stupid" as to leave the car in a vulnerable position in the first place and causing this problem for him. Her very (childhood) fears would have then been confirmed, with George treating her in the same way her parent(s) did. This complication might have led to conflict between Joan and George, and, given enough of these situations, full-fledged marital discord might well have developed.

Because this event was an unusual one, coming completely out of the blue, an impartial observer would clearly see Joan's reaction as way out of proportion. However, Joan quite often has similar, if less obvious, reactions to more ordinary events as well. If she receives a piece of mail from some authority figure, such as the IRS or her ex-husband, Joan is apt to be overcome with fright until she opens the envelope and finds it to be nothing important. She unconsciously expects to be reprimanded in such a situation. A couple of weeks before the incident with the windshield, for instance, Joan had been thrown into a similar panic over a phone call. She had been absent from home for about an hour and, upon returning, had found a message that her mother had called and asked that Joan call her back immediately. Joan quickly put down her bag of groceries and dialed her mother, feeling fearful. When the line was busy, Joan continued to hang up and press the redial button, over and over. She knew she should wait five minutes and try again, but her fear of hearing that she had "done something stupid" was so great she could not. She was driven to find out what her mother wanted, one way or the other. In the meantime, the ice cream was melting.

It's important to recognize that Joan had no control over her reactions to these experiences. Our Western culture is big on believing that it is almost always possible to be in control of ourselves, but the shift of consciousness into a former state, in which problems have not been resolved or grieved, is one area in which our mind is not fully in charge. *We cannot consciously keep this shift from occurring.* What we can do, however, and what we must learn to do if we want to heal, is to become consciously aware that it has happened.

THE CHILDHOOD STATE VERSUS THE ADULTHOOD STATE

The following list can help you develop an awareness of these two states and an ability to distinguish between them. Some common ways of thinking and feeling when in the childhood state are juxtaposed with the probable adult reality with which the person is temporarily out of touch.

CHILDHOOD *Feelings and Statements*	ADULTHOOD *Reality*
"I'll never get over ..."	Everything changes with time.
"I can't stand feeling this way."	If you allow yourself to feel painful or frightening emotions, they will soon pass, leaving you unharmed by the experience.
"Nobody likes me."	Out of the several billion people on this earth, hundreds would probably like you if they met you. Everyone is liked by someone.
"I'll always be alone."	Being alone comes and goes in everyone's lifetime. Most people find themselves alone at some time in their lives, but "always" is seldom the case.
"There is nothing I can do about ..."	There are response options in any situation short of captivity or loss through death.

CHILDHOOD	ADULTHOOD
Feelings and Statements	*Reality*

"Everyone thinks I'm ...
    stupid
    ugly
    crazy
    etc."

Again, with all the people in the world, it is not possible for "everyone" to think any one thing about anyone else.

"I'll die if he or she leaves me."

Yes, it will hurt, but you won't die.

"I shouldn't have made him or her mad."

It is not possible to "make" anyone else feel something. The way people feel is due to the way they are, not something you have done or said.

"I'm not good enough."

Good enough for what? For whom? None of us is wonderful at everything. It shouldn't matter if someone else thinks poorly of you—unless the "something" in question is your job and the "someone" is your boss.

"I'm terrified of ...
    fires
    prowlers
    the dark
    being laughed at
    people behind me
    enclosed places
    not fitting in."

Unless you are in some actual, discernible physical danger—like being in an airplane with engine failure—you are safe.

It seems clear, once we have examined the circumstances, that Joan suddenly found herself in a situation that caused her temporarily to lose her adult state of reality and to think and feel like a child. However, some of the childhood feelings and thoughts in the chart above are such commonly held beliefs that, even as adults, we have come to think of them as true. In other words, the degree to which our whole society is in denial results in a *cultural* state of consciousness that is based on childhood reality. In a sense, *none* of us ever grew up!

The crucial difference between childhood and adulthood is that all children are dependent and almost all adults are independent. It is one thing for a specific event to trigger the unprocessed feelings from an individual's childhood; it is another for almost *everyone* to believe certain things about adult life that are really true only about childhood.

The following charts indicate how certain ways of thinking have evolved from what are actually characteristics of childhood. Characteristics of authentic childhood, and what we should realize from them, are shown for comparison.

CHARACTERISTICS OF CHILDHOOD	CHARACTERISTICS OF ADULTHOOD
The world is small (family).	*The world is full of people.*
("Everyone" and "no one" thinking:)	
If your family doesn't want you, "no one" wants you.	If one person doesn't want you, another will.
If your family disapproves of you, "everyone" disapproves of you.	Someone may disapprove of you, but that is just one person's opinion.
You will die if they don't care.	*You don't need "them" to care.*
("I'll die if" thinking:)	
Life depends on how they feel about you.	With the exception of your employer, what "they" think of you doesn't matter.
Childhood is forever (time distortion).	*Nothing is "forever."*
("Always," "never," and "forever" thinking:)	

CHARACTERISTICS OF CHILDHOOD	CHARACTERISTICS OF ADULTHOOD
If your family doesn't want you, not only does "no one" want you, but you will "never" be wanted by anyone. If your family is critical of you, not only "everyone" disapproves, but they "always" will. *Needs are basic and urgent.*	Everything changes with time. *Everything.* *Basic needs are met by self.*
(Frantic, "do something" thinking:) You are dependent on others for food, physical warmth, and love.	You can provide your own food, physical warmth, shelter, transportation, and you can get along without something when it's absent.
Delay equals danger, feelings of fear and panic. (No perspective.)	Urgency is seldom necessary or appropriate.
Helplessness/Powerlessness.	*You have power.*
("There is nothing I can do," "I have no choice" thinking:) Others control you • Physically (your movements, your ability to explore). • Mentally (what you think). • Emotionally (what you feel). Others control the choices available to you • The nature of your environment (whether it is safe, loving, hostile, punitive, chaotic, orderly, etc.)	You have the right to: • Do with your body as you wish. • Think as you wish. • Have your feelings. • Make choices. Circumstances can limit choices but circumstances change. You create your own environment (select the place, people, atmosphere).

RECOGNIZING SOCIETY'S INACCURATE BELIEFS

Healing work means dealing with each person's very personal childhood experiences. However, the way in which we have all been culturally led to believe that certain realities are "givens"—although they are actually true only of the dependent, childhood state—has also had an important influence on our development. The necessary painful encounters with our own, individual histories will be aided by first understanding that certain societal beliefs we have all accepted as "reality" are not so.

If George leaves Joan as a result of their relationship problems, she will feel the abandonment of the child she was when her parent(s) blamed her instead of comforting her, as well as any other experiences of abandonment that occurred in her childhood. She will cry her heart out and her friends will most likely sympathize with her, agreeing that George has abandoned her and reinforcing the idea that the depth of her trauma is appropriate. If, however, Joan has been doing childhood grief work, she will know that, in fact, what she is feeling is the heartache of her childhood abandonment—that the pain of the loss of George is different from this despair. She will understand that George has not *abandoned* her, as abandonment implies a dependency upon the leaving party that is true only in childhood. What George has done is to *leave*. There is pain when we are left, yes, but abandonment is far more than merely being left.

Joan's friends are apt to disregard anything she says about what her pain really is. After all, we have been conditioned to believe that when we are left—even though we are adults—*it is appropriate to feel abandoned.* Her friends may go further and tell her that her insistence on "dredging up all that childhood stuff" is only making her worse. Even among therapists and counselors, there is limited awareness as to how much of what appears to be pain caused by present events is really old, unprocessed childhood pain. Many will discuss childhood *influences* with their clients but have little understanding of the way in which old pain surfaces in our lives—most likely because few have processed their own histories.

Since confusion can result from engaging in an enterprise that runs counter to the norm in our society, it helps to understand the origins of the concepts that most of us have been conditioned to believe. Part of the healing work, then, must be an ongoing attempt to stay aware of the times when our attitudes are being influenced by this society's conditioning. If we find the cultural reasoning to be faulty, we must refuse to accept it as valid. This requires a willingness to evaluate what we have "always" believed and what others may still believe. Once we come to understand how much of what we have been taught is based on childhood reality, we are free to reject a harmful way of thinking that has been imposed on us and escape its limitations.

PORTRAIT OF AN OVERREACTOR

Personal history work is often begun by people like Joan when they become aware that they periodically overreact emotionally and that these overreactions are often caused by a sense that someone is displeased with them, won't like them, or will think they are stupid.

For Joan, this understanding developed gradually, as she came to see that others did not necessarily react as strongly as she did to certain events or seemed not to need the reassurance and approval that Joan felt she needed. George, as the one closest to her, was the first to call this to her attention. He complained that she was depending on him for things she should be able to do for herself—that sometimes she seemed very needy for his attention, especially when he brought work home. He also pointed out that she often berated herself excessively over small mistakes and then wanted him to reassure her. Joan then began to see other ways in which she acted like a child in looking to George for support, such as when her supervisor said she wanted to see her about something the next day and anxiety kept her from sleeping well. She also began to realize that she felt rejected if someone at work was distracted and did not notice her arrival in the morning, and that she would try to elicit some response from that person later in the day in an attempt to calm her fears. Joan realized that she sometimes burst into tears over some small but unexpected kindness and was unable to understand why she was crying. Her close friends confirmed that she sometimes acted like a needy child and often seemed insecure.

The intensity of these feelings when they were not really warranted was uncomfortable for Joan, and she wanted help with them, but what brought her into therapy was a sense that George was becoming impatient with her. She was concerned for her marriage.

RECOGNIZING UNDERREACTION

Once this work is begun by people like Joan, the very feelings that cause them embarrassment can be used as a tool for getting into the pain of the original abuse experience that has been repressed. And if, like Joan, they seem to be hoping unrealistically to get something from others, that knowledge can be used to relinquish a major defense. But what about people who feel nothing most of the time?

As we've discussed, there seems to be a greater tendency for men to shut down their sensitive feelings than for women, and for women to have exaggerated emotions more often than men. Cultural conditioning obviously has a bearing on this tendency, as is generally borne out by the observation that men are more likely than women to defend against pain by shutting down to feelings. Regardless of the gender of the person, however, and despite the experiential difference in reacting to a given situation by feeling nothing (or less than is appropriate), as opposed to being overcome with excessive emotion, the same shift of consciousness into childhood occurs.

To an observer, this looks very different—Bob, for instance, appeared to be absolutely unaffected by what was happening to his lawn, whereas Joan fell apart when she saw what had happened to her car. Despite appearances, however, both Bob and Joan reacted as the children they once were would have reacted. Bob reacted the way he did when, as a child, he needed to protect himself against acknowledging the painful reality of his childhood: he denied that he had any feelings at all, and thus avoided them completely. When faced with a potentially painful situation in the present, he once again became "the child he was" and used the same defense. In contrast, when Joan's consciousness shifted into childhood, she was assaulted by the childhood panic that preceded her being told how stupid she was; she experienced her feelings, but they were disconnected from their source. When someone like Joan wants to face her childhood pain, the access is through these overreactions—but first, she has to become aware that her feelings are not really a response to present reality, as she thinks. When someone like Bob wants to face his feelings, on the other hand, he must first drop the belief that things don't bother him. Only then will the feelings begin to emerge.

To summarize, one way to know when the old childhood state of consciousness has presented itself is to observe how we handle events that are (or should be) unsettling. For each of us, the predominant tendency should be fairly clear: we are inclined either to be overly emotional or to experience less feeling in response to problems than others seem to. If the latter is true, we may be admired for being so "easygoing" or we may get complaints about being "emotionally closed." Those of us who tend to underreact often have a larger social circle than those who show emotion; our society as a whole finds a lack of emotion more acceptable than blatant expression of feelings. Since this is the case, underreactors may be seen differently depending on the relative closeness of the relationship. Coworkers and bowling buddies may admire us, while longtime friends or loved ones complain. Those of us who feel *more* than is called for are often criticized for being "too sensitive."

When people are not sure which response pattern they tend toward, it can sometimes help to review what others have said about them. The "other" they turn to for this feedback is often the person who is their life/romantic partner or spouse.

The underreactor and overreactor are commonly found to be in relationship with one another. People often think that combination complementary; since one has certain energies the other does not, they can function as "two sides of the same coin." In the long run, however, the pairing is likely to lead to dissatisfaction and disharmony, and the overreactor will be the first to see the marriage counselor.

In addition to using feedback from others in order to get better acquainted with your childhood state, it is a good idea to spend some time noticing your feeling reactions (or lack thereof) to common events, at the same time attempting to determine objectively whether the events in question tallied with your reactions (or lack thereof). Especially for people who overreact more than underreact, understanding the differences between childhood and adult reality and recognizing that some of the feelings culturally accepted as valid for adults actually belong in childhood can help in your self-evaluation.

In a later chapter, you will find a series of exercises designed to help you evaluate your defensive responses. For now, what's important to understand is that both self-observation and understanding of the effects of cultural denial are necessary in order to recognize your own reactions and to begin to know when childhood states of consciousness occur.

chapter four

Overreaction and Underreaction in Concert: The Relationship Link

From the previous descriptions of our shifts into childhood consciousness and how those shifts occur, you might conclude that we are responding this way to random events. While it is true that the repressed feelings and needs of childhood can be aroused haphazardly, that is not usually the case. It is much more likely that old feelings will emerge and defenses will govern our behavior when we are interacting with the people closest to us. In fact, one of the most powerful effects of childhood repression is to influence us to gravitate unconsciously toward the very people who tend to behave in ways that either bring up our repressed emotions or undermine our defenses against them. These are the people we choose for sexual partners or, failing that, for employers.

Whether we are overreactors or underreactors, we tend to be sexually attracted to the very people with whom we will invariably experience interactions that will, in some way, match the aspects of our childhood that were the most painful and unfulfilling. On the surface, this phenomenon may seem outrageously illogical. If, for instance, you spent your childhood with an emotionally distant, unavailable, and critical parent, it would be only sensible to make sure, as an adult, that you looked for someone with different qualities— someone who was warm, caring, supportive, and emotionally open. Conversely, if you defended yourself as a child by disconnecting from your feelings (shutting down), it would certainly seem reasonable for you to choose a partner who did not require you to be open and verbal about feelings. And these are the choices we *would* make—if we were being guided in partner selection by our conscious minds, where our rational processes lie. But it is not the thinking, presently aware part of our minds that motivates us where relationships are concerned; rather, those decisions are made by the unconscious. Thus the effects of our skewed reactions are compounded because we have unconsciously chosen people with whom those problems are most likely to happen.

A CLOSER LOOK AT OVERREACTION

When people overreact to a situation, they tend to exhibit overt behavior. They may become angry, slamming the door on the way out of the house, or become excessively quiet, sinking into an observable pout. Or they may weep or shout, or argue endlessly long after it would be reasonable to give up. Men who overreact often tend toward the former behaviors; women, the latter.

The essence of the childhood defense that the unconscious mind uses to protect the person who overreacts is this: "If I find the right thing to do (or not do, be or not be, etc.) I can change things so I'll get what I need." Although the child may have the emotional and/or intellectual capacity to recognize the hopelessness of the situation, it is too dangerous for him or her to do so. Instead, the child clings to false hope.

We can see, then, that the adult who tends to overreact to situations was a child who repressed the reality that would have led to recognition that any effort to get his or her needs met was useless; and, since such understanding would have been followed by a feeling of hopelessness, he or she also used denial to create a false sense of hope. This hope flew in the face of the reality with which the child could not cope and in fact was designed to substitute for it. False hope formed the basis for the child's unconscious efforts to change the parent(s) to get what he or she needed, and is one way the "false self" expresses itself.

When a child's unconscious continually engages in this maneuver, the unreal hope becomes a permanent part of the child's defensive structure. What was begun in childhood—the unconscious's hopeless project to be whatever was deemed necessary in order to change the parent(s)—continues automatically into adulthood. The child's effort becomes the adult's struggle; and he or she unconsciously chooses people and situations that will enable this struggle to continue.

Again, from a conscious, reasonable point of view, this appears masochistic at best and insane at worst, but neither is the case. The unconscious part of our mind is still in childhood, attempting to meet the *needs of the child we were*—not the wants of the adult we have become. This may sound confusing, since it would be logical to think that the children we were and the adults we are now need the same thing. For instance, an adult whose parent was unavailable and critical may think he needs an available, supportive partner in order to avoid being treated the same way now as he or she was then. It would seem that the child and the adult need the same thing: an available, nurturing person, whether parent or love partner. If we look more closely, however, we will see that *the child's need was for an unavailable, critical parent to become a nurturing, supportive one*. The unconscious is looking to meet the *exact* need of the child. This futile search is the result of the false hope begun as a defense so many years ago, to which it still clings.

As long as repression and denial are operating, the search will continue—meaning that a partner who can help re-create the original conditions will be chosen, so that an effort can be made to change him or her. It also means, of course, that whatever the adult might really want in relationships is superseded by this old need.

A CLOSER LOOK AT UNDERREACTION

Whereas overreaction is often blatant, underreaction is often quite subtle. The partners of people who tend to underreact may suddenly find themselves doing all the talking in what was a dialogue a few minutes earlier. Or they may come home from a dinner party, barely able to make it through the door before exclaiming, "I am furious at Sarah for that insulting remark she made to you, right in front of everyone at the table!" only to be answered by a blank look, then a smile, and "Oh, I didn't think it was so terrible. Would you set up the coffee for the morning?"

People who usually underreact to present-day situations that could potentially threaten their defenses may well, as children, have unconsciously told themselves something on the order of "If I pretend that nothing bad or important is happening here, I can't be hurt."

People with this defense are also protected against feeling hopeless by simply denying that any problem exists. They underreact in an effort to avoid any interactions that would be emotionally uncomfortable. Permitting emotional responses to what other people do or say, or to unfortunate situations of any kind, would be an acknowledgment that these things are important and can hurt. Even though the events take place in the present, any awareness of how they can hurt would threaten to destroy the childhood defense that hides the truth about the past. To make sure this doesn't happen, almost all feeling responses to people and situations must be denied, to ensure against any conflict with others. Underreactors also avoid holding any opinions unacceptable to the majority or, at least, expressing such opinions in certain company. Sometimes the denial of emotions leads to a harboring of resentments that are expressed through chronic irritation over small things or through constant criticisms. Many people for whom emotional shutdown was a childhood defense react with angry outbursts when it is impossible to avoid being affected by someone or something. The reaction is often volatile and frightening but short-lived. Overt anger is the one emotion that the shut-down person may show—especially if that person is a man, since anger in men is socially acceptable. Also, while expressing anger provides relief, it is not an experience of vulnerability or pain, the feelings that are being unconsciously avoided. When a woman is shut down, her expression of anger is likely to be less direct because it is less socially acceptable.

TANDEM REACTIVITY: MARY AND JOE

In the following example, we see how these phenomena might be developed in childhood and expressed later in the lives of two people, Mary and Joe, who meet and become a couple.

Those who know Joe and Mary socially see them as fairly complementary: Joe is a hardworking but easygoing husband and father, while Mary is a warm, sympathetic wife and mother. For their first few years together, things went well. Then two children were born, and though Joe and Mary both worked outside the home, they were able to stagger their hours so that one or the other could always be with the children. It was only after a stressful period of unemployment for Joe that their basic, reactional incompatibility began to show.

If we look beyond Mary's childhood to that of her mother, we see that her mother was raised in an abusive, alcoholic family, and then married a man who drank, thus creating another alcoholic family for Mary and her brothers and sisters. When drinking, her husband often flew into rages, yelling and berating her for being an inadequate wife. Mary's mother, although an adult, responded to these incidents by becoming tearful and apologetic, as she had as a child in response to her father's anger. After such an outburst, Mary's mother typically threw herself into her cooking and housekeeping duties in an attempt to satisfy her husband, all the while appearing to be very sad. The children were ignored during these periods, as well as being unprotected from their father's screaming fits.

Mary was the oldest of three. Though all the children needed their mother to comfort them and make them feel safe, Mary denied this need and repressed the pain of its being unmet. She instead took it upon herself to tend to her younger brothers, telling herself that, at the age of eight, she was old enough to "help" her mother. Mary's helpful behavior went far beyond what would normally be expected from a child "doing her part." Her willingness to go beyond the call of duty indicates that Mary was not simply denying her unmet need but had also developed false hope. Mary's unconscious hope was that if she could tend to the duties that her mother was unable to fulfill, duties that were meant to be undertaken by an adult and that required Mary to give up normal after-school activities, her mother would be less sad, less stressed, and, eventually, more available to nurture Mary. Consciously, Mary felt much older and more capable than her years and had no awareness of either her need or her pain.

The false hope that began with her childhood family's dysfunction continued automatically into Mary's adulthood, developing into what most people saw as her "personality traits" or "nature." As a child, Mary began a project at the unconscious level of her mind—an attempt to get her mother to become able to meet her needs. If someone like Mary does not begin to understand that something other than her own desires is driving her, she will very likely marry a man who expects her to attend to far more than her share of family responsibilities while requiring her to nurture him as well, and to ask for little or nothing for herself. As we will see, this is exactly what Mary has done in marrying Joe.

Someone with Mary's history may well be drawn to an other-centered career, such as nursing or teaching, which gives her little power or authority and offers inadequate compensation—and, in fact, Mary became a nurse. Consciously, she tells herself that helping others is fulfilling and that personal satisfaction is worth more than money. (Many people who choose such professions do so exactly for those reasons—but for Mary, an unconscious factor is operating.) At home, she finds reasons to take on more responsibility than her husband, even though she is exhausted. These reasons are likely to be related to some short-term situation that she expects to improve as some other condition changes (for example, as soon as Joe receives a raise, she will be able to stay home full-time). This expectation is the adult extension of her childhood false hope that her mother would become the strong person Mary needed her to be, just as her rationalizations about her work are the present-day equivalent of the denial of her childhood need for comfort and caring.

Mary's mother had also been unconsciously driven to try to make an angry, alcoholic man—her father—satisfied with her efforts to please him. She, too, was unconsciously motivated to pick such a man to marry so she could continue the efforts begun in childhood to get the love she needed from a father unable to give it. Mary's family history illustrates why dysfunction has been described as intergenerational.

Though Mary is actively engaged in her unconscious attempts to get nurturing through self-sacrifice, she appears to be a sweet, pleasant, and helpful person, emotionally stable. At some point, however, circumstances will likely indicate to her that the returns she has hoped for are not forthcoming, and it is at that point that she will overreact. Such behavior may cause Mary to realize something is wrong. If Mary seeks the help needed to uncover the pain of her childhood, she will not only heal herself so she can discover her true desires and live her adult life according to them, but she will break the chain of repression and denial so that her children can be "real selves."

Now let's consider Mary's husband, Joe. Joe grew up in a family where there were three children, all boys. Joe was the middle child. His father was a small-appliance repairman with his own business, a quiet, mild-mannered man who worked long hours to support the family. Joe's mother stayed home to take care of the children until they were in junior high, and then went to work in an office. There was little emotional closeness in the family. Joe's mother had been raised to believe that, as the only female in the family, it was her job to take care of all the cooking, cleaning, laundry, school lunches, and so forth. She had also grown up in an emotionally bereft family and handled daily life as if everything was matter-of-fact.

When asked about his childhood, Joe remembers that he and his brothers were active in sports after school, busy with homework in the evenings, and, later, that he hung out with the boys and went on dates. He recalls little emotional interaction at home, even between the two parents, but he doesn't think that this was a problem. What Joe doesn't remember is that when something hurt him as a small child, he would cry his heart out but get neither comforting nor even acknowledgment from either of his parents. His father was busy with his business and his mother just went on with what she was doing as if nothing important was happening, and Joe soon came to act as if he had no feelings. It had to be painful for little Joe to be so alone with his hurt, but this was repressed so that he could accept his mother's message: emotional pain is not something to pay any attention to. The next logical extension for Joe's defensive response to make was that nothing was happening worth feeling any pain about.

After Joe's mother went to work in the office, she continued to take care of all the housework as well and was often busy with it late into the night. She never complained, and no one considered that any kind of chore-sharing might be in order. Nothing was expected to bother her, just as nothing was supposed to bother any other family members. When something *did* bother Joe, he felt only a vague, undefined discomfort, in response to which he would shoot baskets or stare into space until he felt OK again. Joe felt best about himself when he was playing basketball and contributing to a winning team; although his parents were usually too busy to attend the games, Joe told himself he "understood." Sometimes he cried at night when he injured himself or the team didn't play well, but he never let anyone know. He thought he shouldn't have painful feelings, so he tried to ignore them; if that wasn't possible, he hid them.

When Joe met Mary, he found he was very comfortable with her. She appeared to be the kind of woman who would be loving and giving without demanding much. Mary, in turn, found herself attracted to Joe, unconsciously sensing that he needed nurturing, which triggered the unconscious "hope" of Mary's childhood—that nurturing would make him more available for intimacy. Consciously, Mary found it easy to overlook Joe's emotional distance, focusing instead on the fact that he was quiet and easygoing, and was not a habitual drinker unlike her angry, alcoholic father. Joe was a carpenter and, with Mary's salary as a nurse, they could afford to get married and start a family. It seemed normal to both that Mary should assume responsibility for all the household needs while also working at a full-time job, just as Joe's mother had done.

When Joe is laid off, as happens sometimes due to the seasonal nature of construction, it does not occur to him to help with the housework or the children on a routine basis. In fact, it would be hard for him to do any of that because when he is unable to work Joe feels the way he did years before when his basketball team lost. He tends to lie around the house, reading, watching television, drinking much more than his usual "after work" beer—anything to take his attention away from the deep sadness threatening to over-whelm him. He becomes irritable and, when he's had too much beer, lashes out angrily at Mary or the children if they need anything from him.

When, after a few weeks of this, Mary begins to suffer from headaches and to feel very tired all the time, she, too, begins to yell at the children when she is feeling "stressed." She feels something is wrong and consults with one of the doctors with whom she works; he thinks she might be depressed. In taking a family history, he concludes that Mary's mother was depressed too, and that there is most likely a tendency to depression in the family genetics. He prescribes mood-elevating medication.

Mary and Joe's problems might be temporarily ameliorated by Mary's antidepressant regime, but unless they look at the fact that Mary consistently engages in destructive self-denial while Joe con-sistently expects that his needs will be met without e.fort on his part—a dynamic that requires neither of them to engage in mutual problem-solving; difficult, heart-felt discussion; or any other form of emotional intimacy—their marriage will die in one way or an-other. Mutual hostility will certainly develop, expressed differently by each of them, but killing the initial attraction.

Often a couple like Joe and Mary will come to realize that antidepressants are not changing anything in a positive way and will seek marriage counseling. This can be a good beginning—if the counselor understands that childhood experiences are at the base of the problem. Improvements are possible, but for each of them the ultimate healing that has the most potential to create a healthy intimacy and blossoming love relationship is found in the regressive work described here.

To summarize, there are two basic ways adults react out of denial of their childhood pain. One way is to underreact, sometimes with underlying rage and sometimes not. The person who does this tends to be male. The other way is to overreact. The person who overreacts, most often female, is generally in some kind of relationship (love or work or both) that she is attempting to change. Both of these reactions originate in the denial defense that the child's unconscious mind used when confronted with a potential awareness of hopelessness.

People's unconscious defensive systems produce inappropriate responses to adult situations in both directions, so that they sometimes react less overtly than is appropriate and sometimes more. The important distinction is that the person who usually underreacts is emotionally shut down (not in touch with any feelings at all, whether appropriate or not, except anger) in order to avoid pain, while the person who overreacts is in touch with feelings but is also actively engaged in an effort to change someone or something outside of herself or himself—against all discouraging evidence of the futility of this attempt. The feelings the overreactor has are actually appropriate to childhood, not to the current struggle; and, for the person who shuts down, the devastating pain that is being avoided also belongs to childhood, not to whatever is happening now (although, consciously, he feels little or nothing).

The shut-down underreactor, then, is "avoiding," while the overreactor "struggles." There is a relationship between these distorted reactions, avoidance and struggle, in that each person is attracted to the other because of an unconscious drive to get old childhood needs met. The struggler is driven to find someone like Mom or Dad in order to try to change them, while the avoider looks for someone who is capable of nurturing with warmth and caring and will expect little or nothing in return.

These unconscious drives cause us to be drawn to people and other significant life situations (jobs, for example, or places to live) without any real understanding of what the source of the attraction truly is. We end up re-creating the abusive aspects of our childhoods with no awareness that this is happening.

It is this unconscious re-creation that causes us so much misery—and yet it is this very phenomenon that also provides us with potential for healing. Once we understand how our unconscious minds have used repression and denial to protect us and why we needed that protection and have some idea of how our adult reactions have been distorted as a result, we are closer to having the tools to realize that healing potential.

We will next examine how these same dynamics operate to unconsciously influence us in our choice of profession or place of employment.

chapter five

Overreaction and Underreaction in the Workplace

As we have seen, people who have been abused in childhood are often attracted to the very people and situations that trigger their over- or underreaction. Many may be drawn to spouses or romantic partners who evoke the struggle or shut-down response; others over- or underreact in the workplace. In fact, unconscious parent/child interactions are common in the workplace and can be seen in things like procrastinating with the work of a boss you don't like even though doing so can jeopardize your job, competing with a co-worker who seems to be "favored" by the employer, or giving overly complimentary evaluations to employees because you're afraid of their anger.

Interestingly, while most of the problems occur when employees stay stuck in untenable or outgrown positions, or continue working for abusive bosses, it's not uncommon for employers to be unable to resolve difficult work situations because they are over- or underreacting to their subordinates.

MARSHA'S STORY

Marsha is a thirty-five-year-old C.P.A. working in the accounting
department of a manufacturing company, and she hates her job. It's
not the actual work she minds—in fact, she *likes* the work a good
deal—it's her colleagues and her boss who make her not want to go
to work each morning. Her boss, Ted, frequently acts as if something were wrong with her work; he frowns, sounds exasperated, or
gives irritable replies to Marsha's questions, as if to suggest that she
should already know the answers. Donna, a coworker of much
longer tenure than Marsha, makes a point of implying that Ted is
unhappy with Marsha about one thing or another. Marsha thinks she
should ask Ted whether he is dissatisfied with her work, but she's
afraid to; she does not like confrontation, and would prefer to avoid
it. She hopes to solve the problem by performing so well that no one
could complain.

While browsing through the self-help section of a bookstore,
Marsha discovers that she fits the profile of a "co-dependent." She
decides that joining a CODA group might help her become more
self-confident and better at dealing with people and situations she
fears. To put into practice what she is learning at CODA, Marsha
steels herself to approach Ted directly, in spite of her fears. For a
while she does this with some regularity, always getting the answer
that he *is* satisfied—yet Donna keeps suggesting otherwise and Ted
keeps frowning. In fact, Ted has been anywhere from annoyed to
angry at being asked. Finally Marsha decides to ask for a written
evaluation to solve the problem, only to have Ted snarl at her, "I
told you you're doing a good job—what's your problem?" At this
point, Marsha gives up asking, although she continues to wonder if
her work is unsatisfactory.

Donna and Florence, the woman who answers the office phone,
also behave in ways that make Marsha uncomfortable. Since Donna
and Florence socialize together, their conversations regularly leave
Marsha out. They also tend to cast disparaging glances at Marsha's
clothing as if to say "Who dressed you this morning?"

From the moment she was hired Marsha has been afraid of not

being liked—being laughed at behind her back or thought stupid. Early on, she developed the habit of closely scrutinizing her clothing and general appearance in the mirror before leaving home in the morning, to make sure there was nothing that anyone could laugh at. At work, she tends to be as silent as possible to protect herself from saying anything that could be considered stupid. Constantly obsessing about what others might be thinking about her, she does not interact with her office mates in the way most people do, and often finds herself missing what's going on. Commonly, she won't know a joke has been told until she hears the laughter, and then she doesn't dare to ask about it for fear—again—of being thought stupid.

JON'S STORY

Jon, a forty-two-year-old package-delivery-truck driver, complains about his job every day. The work is physically taxing and the company for which he works expects greater speed than is reasonable. Jon feels constant pressure to work faster despite the unavoidable delays of traffic and having to wait for signatures. He whines routinely, but finds fault with anyone who suggests that the company is being unfair, defending its need for a good profit margin. He ignores any suggestions friends make about looking for a different job.

DORA'S STORY

Dora is a thirty-eight-year-old manager with a degree in business. She works for a midsize corporation and loves her job, but finds it so exhausting that she can barely keep up with her housekeeping chores on the weekend. Although she lives alone and has only herself to care for, Dora finds that Friday evenings bring on a sudden physical and mental "letdown," and all she wants to do is lie around her apartment and read.

Dora's weekend lassitude is in stark contrast to the whirlwind of energy she displays at work, and even on weekday evenings. She has a responsible position with her company and is renowned for her ability to accomplish a lot in a short time. She gets positive feedback from her supervisor and has been promoted twice; her semiannual job-performance evaluations have mentioned only small items as needing improvement.

The one thing that bothers Dora is that she receives a somewhat lower salary than other managers with similar responsibilities. She knows that this is because she was hired at a time when the company was restructuring and doing very little hiring; she was lucky to get the job at all. Dora realizes she needs to address the problem with her supervisor and feels confident that she will get a good response, but she keeps putting it off, continuing meanwhile to feel treated as "less than" the others. In addition, despite all evidence to the contrary, Dora feels as if she is "not doing well enough and needs to try harder." She feels a "push" from inside her to "do more, do better, do more, do better, do, do, do, do."

ARTHUR'S STORY

Arthur is a twenty-five-year-old office worker at a small nonprofit arts organization. He likes his job, but feels insecure about keeping it. Although his work is satisfactory, a conflict has developed between him and his supervisor, Nadine, dating back to his questioning her about rules concerning pay schedules, vacation and sick time, bonuses, evaluation policies, notice required when quitting, etc. When Arthur has needed sick time or personal leave, his requests are sometimes granted cheerfully and generously ("Take all the time you need," "Don't worry about it") and, at other times, not ("What is it *this* time?"). Sometimes he has had to use vacation time for these needs. His fellow employees don't seem to know what the policies are either.

When Arthur asked to see the personnel policies, he was told that they had not been put in writing and that the board of directors decided these policies, which changed depending on the success of their fund-raising efforts. Nadine told Arthur she would answer his questions as they arise and as she is informed by the board. This left Arthur feeling more vulnerable to his supervisor's power than he thought reasonable, but he didn't see what he could do about it. Subsequently, whenever he attempted to object to something he felt was not being done the way it should be, he was called a "troublemaker" and found himself scapegoated. The situation became even more upsetting to Arthur when he discovered some board minutes discussing the availability of funds for staff salary increases; yet, months later, only Nadine's salary had been increased.

CONSCIOUS AND UNCONSCIOUS MOTIVES

The same unconscious motives that operate when we choose sexual/love partners can also operate when we choose a career, decide to accept or reject a job offer, or stay in a job in which we are not reasonably content. However, because all adults need to generate income on which to live (whereas adults do not *need* to be in a love relationship), the reasons for accepting or staying in a job we don't like may simply be practical. On the other hand, it's clear that those of us who developed the (false) hope of changing someone through our actions (and later are subject to overreaction) or who believed that painful truth could be escaped through denial (and later are subject to underreaction) are not only likely to be unconsciously influenced in our choice of career, but are likely to accept or continue to work in job situations that are unpleasant, unfulfilling, or even abusive.

A CLOSER LOOK

When we examine the situations facing Marsha, Jon, Dora, and Arthur, we find that they contain elements of practical considerations but also reveal unconscious influences from their childhood histories and defenses. We see that overreaction and underreaction, along with old hope and avoidance, are present. Marsha and Dora are both college-educated women with degrees in the field of their choice—accounting and business, respectively.

As Marsha's support group and friends were not enough help for her, she sought counseling. In discussing her history, she discovered that she was the scapegoat in the family of her childhood. Her father often laughed at her and called her "stupid" when she made common mistakes. The rest of the family, happy that his derision had been deflected from them, joined in. Marsha really felt safe only when alone, so she sought refuge from the abuse by retreating to her room. At the same time, she denied that her father was cruel, and consciously admired him as a successful businessman. Marsha always hoped she could somehow please him. When she decided to become an accountant, she was affected by two unconscious influences: to work at something that she thought would require minimal contact with people (so she could feel "safe") and to become successful at something that she hoped would win her father's approval. Although Marsha's father died a few months before she took her present job, Marsha was still unconsciously attempting to win his approval. In this case, choosing a "people-less" career that related to business made for a combination of avoidance (seeking solitude for "safety") and hope (trying to please her businessman father—to show him she is not "stupid").

Dora's history involved being the child who didn't "fit in." She couldn't "take things in stride" like her three siblings and was more emotional and needy. Her parents were committed to presenting a picture of the "perfect family," but in reality her father was a quiet alcoholic who had occasional, very secret extramarital affairs, while her mother attempted to fulfill her unmet needs for intimacy through activities with her children. The household was a busy one, with everyone always engaged in some kind of "fun" activity, apparently "happy." There was no room for anger or sadness, or, actually, the reality of the relationships. Because Dora had trouble pretending, she was often disapproved of and came to feel that she was not as good as the others or as well liked. She blamed herself, but never gave up thinking she could "do better" to win their acceptance and love. It was natural for Dora to pick a career in business, with medium- to large-size companies, since success there would require both competitiveness and "fitting in."

Unconsciously, both Marsha and Dora chose careers that would enable them to continue the effort to fulfill the false hope of their childhoods, and jobs where they would be faced with situations to which they would respond defensively, either over- or underreacting when threatened. Their work situations would also resemble their families of origin insofar as Marsha and Dora would once again encounter difficult experiences. Either abuse in some form would actually be present, or situations would exist that could cause abuse to be perceived.

As neither Jon nor Arthur was a college graduate, the type of employment they sought depended in part on their previous experience, such as part-time jobs during high school. Since Arthur had previous office work and computer experience, the job at the nonprofit organization was something for which he qualified. Jon, on the other hand, had been raised on a ranch and was accustomed to outdoor work and lifting heavy items. Driving a truck seemed right to him. It is unlikely that any unconscious motivation was involved in Jon's and Arthur's job choices, based as they were on the men's skills and the environments in which they feel comfortable. However, since Arthur finds himself confronting problems that appear to be abusive and are affecting his emotional well-being, and neither is handling his situation effectively, it is likely that the defensive reactions of childhood are influencing their responses to job-related problems.

Jon's father's ranch carried a heavy load of debt and depended upon the winter snowpack for water. There was never a year when it was not operating on a slim financial margin. As the only boy in the family, Jon was called on to help outside year-round from the time he was very small. The situation worsened when Jon was in high school and his father went to work in the city. This had the positive effect of providing a steady income for the family, but it meant that most of the ranch work fell to Jon, who was physically mature but also busy with school and the social needs of a teenager. He was invariably very tired at suppertime, and totally exhausted by bedtime. Thus we see that Jon's childhood was spent in a situation in which his needs were unimportant, in which his reason for being seemed to be to generate income for others. Whenever friends who lived in town suggested that his father was being unfair or was robbing Jon of the fun of being on the football team, Jon hotly disagreed, telling them they just didn't understand anything about ranching.

Arthur's problems were different. His parents were members of a religious cult, whose activities were always secret and sometimes illegal. He has few memories of his childhood, only a vague sense that some kind of "mystery" surrounds it. He always felt "different" in school and had few playmates. As an adult, Arthur wakes in terror from occasional dreams of large nighttime gatherings and strange, shadowy activities. As soon as he graduated from high school he moved several hundred miles away from his parents and is reluctant to visit them, although he does so whenever he feels he "should." They are very nice to him, calling often, writing, sending money when he has extra expenses, and expressing interest in his life. Arthur wonders why he feels uneasy with and about them. His life goes well generally, although his relationships with women don't last and he periodically finds himself embroiled in some social, political, or workplace turmoil around issues of honesty and fairness. If he thinks someone is lying or being secretive, he immediately leaves the situation, since he has a very powerful urge to smash something or, worse, beat up someone. He knows that he shouldn't let these things bother him to such an extent and that his reactions are way out of proportion. When he gets involved in a verbal confrontation, he finds he cannot stay out of it even when he stands to lose something important to him—his job, for instance—but he has never known why.

STANDING STILL FOR ABUSE

When we examine the work situations of each of these people, we can see that there are clearly abusive elements in all but Dora's. We can also see that each person, including Dora, is reacting with the under- or overreaction defenses he or she used (unconsciously) in childhood as protection from abusive family realities.

Marsha's boss does not relate to his employees in an above-board, straightforward manner and, when questioned, gets angry. He makes statements that contradict his body language and that cannot be relied on as truth. This is abusive, but Marsha prefers to believe that the fault for the discrepancy belongs instead to her coworkers. In fact, her coworkers are also abusive, treating her in a way that excludes her. Although it is true that Marsha made an awkward entrance into the department because of her tendency to isolate herself out of fear of being thought stupid, she has been working diligently in therapy to change the behavior that contributes to the present mistreatment. Unfortunately, both Florence and Donna continue to enjoy themselves at Marsha's expense. (Marsha's behavior exhibits a combination of underreaction—to her boss—and overreaction, albeit subtle and hidden, to her coworkers.)

Dora's situation may not be abusive at all, due to the fact that the only external sign that she is being denigrated is the discrepancy in her salary as compared to others. There is a reason for that, however, and if Dora takes action to address the problem, it may be corrected. She has every reason to believe she would get a positive response to a request for a raise, so it is probable that all of her drive to perform and her feelings of being "less than" are coming from her own history. Dora is driven by hope, unconsciously attempting to find in her work environment the "belonging" and approval that were missing from her childhood. Ironically, she *does* belong and she *is* approved of; but because her efforts are aimed at fixing the past, she is not able to sense this. Instead, she thinks she must keep trying to get it, and she focuses on the one factor that *could* indicate that "they" don't think she's "as good as" the others. (Dora is clearly overreacting.)

The company Jon works for expects unreasonable performance from its drivers, considering its profit margin more important than the well-being of its employees. His employers are taking advantage of Jon in the same way his father did when he was younger. Now, as then, the work exhausts him, but, unlike then, he has the option of at least looking for other employment. Without any conscious awareness, Jon thinks and feels like the child he once was, feels helpless to change the situation, and fully believes that there is good cause for it. When he complains of fatigue, and someone criticizes his employers in response, he defends them, saying it's really not a problem. (An underreaction.)

Arthur can figure out what is going on at the Arts Center and knows there is little he can do about "making it right," but he stays on because he needs the job, does it well, and it supports him; he also likes many of his coworkers. With a different history, it would be possible for Arthur to approach his boss with needs and problems in a way that would facilitate a positive response. Or he could live with the salary freeze while keeping an eye out for another, better-paying job. For Arthur, however, this isn't easy. He feels furious over Nadine's lack of honesty and fairness. It "isn't right," and Arthur cannot help doing and saying things that agitate the situation. Although he knows that Nadine is becoming impatient with his behavior, he can't seem to stop himself. (Overreaction.)

We can see that in each of these four people, unconscious influences are operating as a result of the original need to protect themselves from knowing about and feeling the effects of the abuse they experienced as children. Each is influenced in some way with regard to his or her employment—either in career choice, or in using old, defensive responses to workplace problems, or both.

BOSSES WITH SKEWED REACTIONS

Employers as well as employees are unconsciously influenced in the workplace. Decisions on hiring, firing, promotions, and workplace discipline may also be affected by the childhood history of the employer. Rob, who supervises twelve people in the training department of a major bank, has two employees who require his continuous support to perform adequately. He has supervised them for three years, with no real improvement. Two superiors have suggested independently that Rob transfer them to different departments where they might be more effective, but he has not. Instead, he spends extra time with them, attempting to engineer a success that he unconsciously sees as proof of his value.

Rob, an only child, was unwanted from the beginning and treated as superfluous. More than anything, he wanted to be able to make an important contribution—to be needed, to be seen as useful and capable. These two employees are the most recent of a long series of lost causes he has tried to turn around. Using his position as a supervisor, Rob has unconsciously been attempting to get his childhood need met.

There are many ways in which repressed childhood experiences can unconsciously influence employers to hire the wrong people, keep the wrong people, and fire the wrong people. For instance:

- An employer who comes from a family in which promises were made but rarely kept, where needs were considered unimportant and ignored, may well be unconsciously influenced to hire incompetent employees with authority problems, thus re-creating the employer's family history.
- An employer who was made to feel stupid as a child may unconsciously feel threatened by an exceptionally bright employee. Perhaps imagining that others have noticed the employee's intelligence and considered the employer dull by comparison, the employer may find a way to get rid of the bright employee.
- An employer who had a parent who was emotionally unstable to the point of being unable to function—perhaps even hospitalized—may well have grown up feeling responsible and might have trouble firing any employee who appeared to be unable to handle the job loss.

SAFETY FIRST

We can also see the influence of unconscious defenses when we stay with jobs we should leave. Perhaps our boss is abusive, perhaps we are underpaid—yet we find excuses to stay. Barbara, for instance, came from a family in which her parents were needy, desperate people. She felt guilty when she left to go to school, and when she decided to take a job across the country, she had to fight the feeling that she was abandoning them. As it turned out, she found a job where her employers were very similar to her

parents—inadequate in running their business and happy to depend on her by giving her major, time-consuming responsibility
with little pay. After a couple of years, Barbara realized that the
job was a dead end, yet she was unable to leave; feelings of guilt
and panic overtook her whenever she seriously considered it.
When her friends told her she should look for something better,
she replied that she found the responsibility a challenge, and that
when she was ready to move on, she would.

Of course, some people are stuck in jobs they don't like and
would leave if they could but have realistic financial reasons for
staying. Barbara's panicky feelings, on the other hand, were caused
unconsciously by her childhood fear that her parents wouldn't survive without her help—and then who would take care of her? Barbara badly needed to be able to act in her own best interest despite
these fears, as she had done when she left for school and moved
across the country. (Better yet, she needed to do the personal history work of regressive therapy so she would stop re-creating this
situation.)

Decisions about leaving jobs can be very difficult because our
fears are not always based on childhood reality but may be true in-
dicators that an unconsidered action, such as surrendering our
source of income without having secured another, can truly hurt us.
On the other hand, many of our fears are *not* "real"—instead, they
are signs that the vulnerability we felt as children has been unconsciously carried over into our adulthood. We "attach" those fears to
the present situation so they can seem to be rational.

These fears are quite commonly attached to money, which as
adults we really do need to survive. Money, after all, buys food,
clothing, shelter, and transportation—the basics we all need. Thus
the financial fear generated by the thought of quitting a job without having another is real. However, when someone with a comfortable investment income resists making reasonable spending
decisions that are recommended by her or his financial adviser out
of fear of "going broke," we can safely assume that money has unconscious significance, with some repressed childhood fear attached to it.

Let's look at another example of the influence of unconscious childhood defenses on on-the-job behavior. Sandy, an assistant to a freelance photographer, struggled for months with her employer, who never seemed satisfied with her work. Yet Sandy felt he gave her inadequate direction and was unfair in his criticisms. Though it was clear that they were not a good match of employer and employee, Sandy did not look for another job. Influenced by her childhood experiences of being the powerless victim of her parents' complaints—she could never satisfy her critical mother, and her father would not allow Sandy to be hurt or angry with his wife—she retaliated for her employer's unjust criticisms in passive-aggressive ways. Sandy took long lunch breaks, complained about her boss to other staff members, did her work carelessly, and rolled her eyes at him when she thought he wasn't looking, leading inevitably to her being fired without having another position lined up. Because she was waging an unconscious war, Sandy did not recognize the self-destructiveness of her actions—and even when she was dismissed, she saw it as just another unfair act on her employer's part.

As we will discuss later in greater detail, most of the time our fears about safety are unwarranted in present reality. But we must use caution in handling our work situations because our first priority must be to ensure our own safety when it really is the issue regardless of whatever unconscious influences may also be present.

In our work lives, as in our intimate relationships, we are either unconsciously drawn to the very situation that will, in some way, re-create the abusive environment of our childhoods, or we will automatically interpret and react to situations as we did as children. We are then unable to process our experience in an effective way, and may increase the difficulty of our employment situation.

People need help to feel, know, and understand what happened to them as children, no matter how painful and difficult that may be, in order to break free of the grip of denial. Unless we squarely face the old reality, and are willing to feel the pain of it, we can never stop protecting ourselves in nonproductive ways. Recognizing useless or even destructive behavior will not be enough to change it. Childhood healing work must be done.

The next few chapters will show how.

chapter six

Identifying Your
Symbols and
Triggers

In the previous two chapters we discussed the unconscious drive that draws us to people and situations in our adult lives that will re-create the abusive aspects of our childhoods. This is the psyche's attempt to solve our old problems. Unfortunately, we cannot solve these old problems, since they do not exist in adult reality. (Actually, we could never have solved these problems, even during childhood when they did exist, because we were powerless children.)

THEN VERSUS NOW

We have seen that the repression of childhood trauma and abuse has led to the widespread belief that certain things that are really true only about our lives as children, with our parents or other adults in control of us, are true about adult life as well (Chapter Three). Thus, what we consider "normal" responses to difficult events in our lives may actually be completely out of context; they may be perfectly appropriate to certain unfelt events of our childhoods, but are not at all the responses we would now make were it not for repression and

denial. Whether we over- or underreact to a present experience, we
are still acting as if it were so powerful that we must defend ourselves against its full impact. We often hear—and may ourselves
make—statements like "I couldn't handle that" or "That would kill
me" or "Don't tell her that, it could destroy her" or "I can't live
without him" or "This is too hard, I can't stand it" or "I am too
afraid to. . . ." All these statements actually refer to realities of
childhood, when certain truths and experiences *were* too much for
us to bear. So we didn't. We repressed them. Now, when something
happens that breaks through the repression and forces us to experience the original feelings, that old reality comes with it. We do not
realize that what we are feeling belongs to our childhoods, or that
the way we are interpreting our present situation does also. As both
of these things are unrecognized, we believe that what was true then
is true now.

We have been unable to put those pieces of our pasts where they
belong—in our conscious memories—because we were unable to
process the experiences fully when they occurred. Our minds have the
capacity to process experiences that happened long ago, but when our
defense mechanisms continue to function as if "then" is "now," *without our being aware of it,* we cannot utilize that ability.

In order to develop an awareness of our defense mechanisms,
we must first begin to recognize when we are overreacting, or
struggling with something or someone, and when we are shutting
down, or *avoiding pain.* There are usually patterns to this activity.
In other words, if you observe yourself closely, you will find that
you frequently tend to react in some "old" way to certain people
or situations.

I call such behavior "old" because it is really a childhood defense maneuver. It is crucial to understand that struggle and avoidance are not just bad habits that can be dropped but are, to the
unconscious mind, survival tactics. Since this is the case, we cannot
change these behaviors merely by reminding ourselves what to stop
or start doing. When certain responses have been unconsciously
"coded" as necessary to protect the life of the organism, it takes
work *at the unconscious level* to change the power behind the drive

to engage in these responses. We may be very well-meaning and committed to change—we may be loaded with "willpower"—but all those qualities are dependent upon the activity of the conscious mind, and our conscious mind is not in charge of these behaviors. The belief that we can change our behavior if we "know" where the problem comes from can lead to frustration and self-criticism when, despite our best (conscious) efforts, the behavior doesn't change. In some way we are all like Arthur, who understands that it would be best for him to stay out of disputes at work but "can't help himself." To be able to truly help ourselves, we must work where the problem comes from—the unconscious. We can begin by understanding what "old" behaviors really are and recognizing the aspects of our lives that tend to trigger these behaviors.

DEFENSIVE SYMBOLS

Whenever we find that we are continually defensive with certain people (struggling or avoiding), this should indicate to us that these are the people to whom we have been unconsciously drawn as representatives of the childhood reality we couldn't face. They become *symbolic* in the sense that we project onto them the qualities of our old situation, and react *now* in whatever way we learned to defend ourselves *then*. Those who protected themselves against entrenched painful reality by unconsciously believing they had the power to change it undertake adult struggles, while those whose defense was to shut down continue to do so.

STRUGGLING

We have already discussed children who give up their natural way of being to attempt to become whatever they think will please their parents. A quiet boy who loves to read may instead become active in Little League and learn to walk and talk in a "tough" way. A bubbly girl with a natural talent for drama and humor may turn into a concerned and serious child who takes care not to "disturb" the parents who are busy with some problem that leaves no time for her and who disapprove of her exuberance. Both children secretly hope that their adaptive behavior will bring them the caring and attention they need.

The childhood adaptation becomes an adult struggle because the need for caring, attention, support—whatever it is in a particular case—is never met, and the attempt to get it by pleasing someone else is unconscious. The false hope created by the unconscious prevents us from knowing and feeling the hopelessness of the situation. This program automatically continues into adulthood so that the hope can stay alive, a continuation of the protection that was needed in childhood but is no longer necessary.

A struggle can be recognized when a person continues to attempt to make something happen although there is little or no probability of success. It's interesting how many of our common sayings reflect an awareness of this struggle at the level of folk wisdom. An adult who is struggling to get an old need met in a symbolic way is sometimes seen to be "beating his head against a stone wall" or "trying to make a silk purse out of a sow's ear."

The most common struggles take place in relationships, but they can sometimes be undertaken with situations, as we saw Rob doing in the previous chapter. You may remember that he was attempting (unconsciously) to improve the work performance of his inadequate employees in order to prove his own worth (to his parents). There was ample evidence that it wasn't going to happen, yet he kept trying. Another example might be someone who is determined to become a scientist in spite of having little aptitude for math.

Still another example can be seen in the cases of two of my clients, Mark and Helga. Each came from a family in which neglect was a primary theme. Their parents really didn't want to have to take care of or to be responsible for their children. Some children from this type of situation will respond by becoming abnormally "independent" at an early age, thereby losing touch with their neediness. Mark and Helga, however, did the opposite. In an unconscious attempt to "force" someone—their parents—to take care of them, neither ever quite learned to manage his or her own life. For

Mark and Helga, this mismanagement of their personal lives involved struggling with situations, because as long as they were inadequately cared for, they could maintain the false hope that someone would step in (as their parents should have).

Years ago I had a "Peanuts" cartoon on the wall of my office waiting room. The cartoon featured a discussion between Linus and Charlie Brown. Linus says that he has "found the secret to contentment"—to accept every day just as it is and not worry about tomorrow. Charlie Brown objects, "No, no, we can't do that. I'm still trying to make yesterday better!" When we do this—and, prior to undertaking healing work, we all do—we are struggling.

AVOIDING

When emotional withdrawal is used instead of struggling, it can be obvious, as in a situation where one person wants to talk things out and the other person won't—doesn't agree that there is anything to talk about, thinks such discussion is silly, or simply leaves, making himself or herself unavailable. Withdrawal can also be more subtle, as when the person *seems* available—is pleasant, gregarious, and conversational—but "goes blank" when interaction becomes emotionally uncomfortable, and is unable to relate to people at a deeper level.

In the discussion that follows, I use the masculine pronoun for the emotionally shut-down person and the feminine pronoun for the person who is struggling to get something that is not available. I want to stress again that this does not mean that *all* men are shut down and *all* women struggle, since that is not the case. However, the first type of defense is more commonly found among men, the second more commonly found among women. These two types also tend to be attracted to one another and to end up in relationships together.

THE MARRIAGE NEXUS: BRIAN AND KATHY

The following examples will show how each type can originate, the subtle and obvious forms of withdrawing, and the way in which the avoider and the struggler are attracted to one another:

Brian, who had an alcoholic father, became a "nice guy" who couldn't respond to emotionally painful situations. His father, Curt, was a hard worker who liked to come home to cocktails, a late dinner, and the undivided attention of his wife. Although not an alcoholic herself, Carole, Brian's mother, gladly joined Curt for cocktails. To arrange for the quiet time together that her husband wanted, she fed the children before he came home and sent them to bed at an abnormally early hour.

Brian repressed his anger at his father's dominance of his mother's attention, his frustration at lying awake for the hour or more it took him to fall asleep, and his feelings of abandonment by both of them. As an adult, he remembered only family outings, his mother's warmth when his father wasn't present, and his father's interest in his school's activities.

In relation to his wife and children, Brian appeared warm and caring, yet habitually manipulated the situation so that, whenever possible, the children were excluded when he was with his wife.* Brian was completely unaware that anything was amiss—and was puzzled and irritated when his children complained about having to wait to get help with their schoolwork or to ask a question. He felt their demands were unreasonable and told them so. Similarly, if his wife, Kathy, asked for Brian's support in dealing with a family matter, he would fail her at the crucial time because he was unable to grasp the significance of the interaction.

One continuing problem involved Brian's parents, Curt and Carole, with whom the couple socialized frequently. Brian had divorced his first wife to marry Kathy, and this was not a welcome

---

*It is important to note that, although this behavior was the same as that of his father, it was *not* the result of "role modeling," as is so often thought. Brian's actions originated with his *childhood need* for the undivided attention of his mother; his wife became an unconscious symbol for her.

event for Curt and Carole. In addition, through therapy Kathy had become independent and outspoken; when something bothered her, she addressed it. Curt and Carole were not comfortable with confrontation, preferring to ignore any difficulties in relating—one major reason that Brian was so "nice" and missed conflicts in interactions. Kathy was not their favorite person, as had been clear to her from their behavior, tone of voice, and facial expressions. In group interactions, she was frequently ignored, her suggestions disregarded. Sometimes Carole even acted as if she hadn't heard a direct question from Kathy.

Since Kathy was becoming less and less comfortable with these family gatherings, she and Brian discussed possible solutions to the problem. She asked him to support her when Carole was on her worst behavior. For instance, if Carole totally disregarded Kathy's input when several family members were making a decision together, Kathy wanted Brian to intervene to say something like "Mom, didn't you hear what Kathy just said?" Brian readily agreed to do so, expressing his own anger at his mother's treating his wife in that way. They also discussed the idea of meeting privately with Carole and Curt to talk about the matter directly and openly, if indirect action didn't change anything.

It took several of these episodes before Brian was able to see and hear these things as they happened, even though he had appeared to look for them. After each event, Kathy would go over the conversation in detail, pointing out Carole's put-downs. At first, Brian could see them only in retrospect, although he was later able to see and act during the family activity.

Brian and Kathy did finally sit down with Carole and Curt to have a conversation about Carole's behavior and Kathy's feelings, since Brian's supportive behavior hadn't made any difference. During this confrontation, Carole completely denied that the behavior Kathy was complaining about had ever occurred, suggesting instead that Kathy was "too sensitive and somewhat paranoid"—all said in a very "nice" way. Although Brian had expressly wanted the meeting to include him and his father, who Brian felt was somehow supporting Carole's abusiveness, and although he wanted to support

Kathy in the confrontation, he sat quietly throughout it, looking pleasant and saying little. When questioned later by Kathy, for whom the meeting had been of no benefit, Brian said he had "not noticed" his mother's statements or her denial of her actions—only how "nice" she had seemed. Since this was the case, he had not been moved to say anything himself.

His experiences with Kathy, coupled with his failure to grasp the significance of the children's feelings when their needs for attention weren't met, illustrate Brian's denial of his own feelings and his inability to connect with any of the painful emotions of his family.

Brian's wife, Kathy, had a rejecting, critical father who was unhappy in his marriage and had never achieved the level of financial success that he wanted. He hated his job, felt exploited by his wife, and was angry at life in general. He was a self-centered man, absorbed in his own discontent to the point that he had no ability to nurture his children; actually, he was emotionally needy, and perceived himself as an abused victim (his *own* childhood legacy). Kathy was a sensitive child, who felt her father's unhappiness intuitively. There was no way she could get what she wanted from him, but her unconscious denied the hopelessness of her situation and drove her to try to be good enough to make him happy (and therefore capable of nurturing her). She would do anything to please him, including some of the "grown-up" things her mother should have been doing, such as asking him how his day had been and bringing him a drink. To be available for these things, she denied her childhood need to play with her friends and repressed her pain about what she wasn't getting: parents who were interested in how *her* day had gone.

Brian later became the symbol with whom Kathy could continue her childhood struggle. He fit her unconscious drive perfectly, since he, like her father, seemed to need someone's attention to "make him happy." Because of this dynamic, of which neither Brian nor Kathy was consciously aware, when Brian failed to understand the appropriateness of his children's protests, Kathy could not respond to them either.

JULIE AND PETER

While Brian's defenses developed one way, his sister Julie's developed in another. Julie was afraid of noises and shadows during those early bedtime hours and would cry for Mom or Dad, hoping thereby to elicit their missing love and attention. When they did come, it was only in anger at having been interrupted. She soon learned to cry quietly and endure her fear alone.

As an adult, Julie married Peter, an emotionally shut-down man who liked to spend time in solitary pursuits—working late, reading, going hunting on weekends, or watching sports events for hours. Peter's childhood contained a number of elements found quite often in men who are obviously shut down. Peter, the oldest of three children, had two younger sisters. His father was also a distant, emotionally unavailable person, and his mother felt deprived of the attention and affection she had expected to get from her husband (a continuation of *her* childhood history). Life in her family taught her to keep painful feelings to herself, so she had become someone who suffered quietly, only half aware that she was feeling bad. Those around her, however, could sense intuitively that she needed to be nurtured. With the openness of a child, Peter was especially sensitive to this need; at the same time, his mother turned to him, the oldest child and a boy, for some of the emotional gratification that was unavailable from her husband. Beginning when Peter was five or six years old, she would often confide in him some of the things she had done or a problem she'd had that day. If Peter had been aware of his feelings at that time, he would have found that he became vaguely anxious when walking home after school in anticipation of having to bear the responsibility of his mother's neediness. Instead, he repressed this and began to seek outside activities, spending as little time at home as possible. Thus Peter became a man who unconsciously felt the need to escape from any intimacy with his wife, since intimacy symbolized to him the inappropriate neediness of his mother. Julie was a perfect symbol, since what seemed to her to be a desire for adult closeness was actually *her* unmet childhood neediness. It was logical that this would arouse Peter's defenses, as it would be perceived as the same sort of threat to his integrity that his mother's behavior had been.

Of course, neither of them was aware of any of this, and Julie was upset by Peter's emotional and physical unavailability, seemingly for both herself and the children. Sometimes she cried, thinking about her husband, when in fact she was really feeling the hurt from the mistreatment of her childhood. At other times she went on the offensive, berating Peter and lecturing him about his duties as a proper spouse and father. When Julie cried, Peter acted as if he didn't notice how she was feeling, and stayed engrossed in his sports or his paper. When she stormed at him, he would stalk out of the house, sometimes not returning for hours, or yell at Julie, telling her that she wanted too much from him. They fought a lot and wondered whether they should get a divorce.

The personalities of Brian and Peter and the way they defended themselves against feeling were different, despite the fact that neither could deal with emotional pain. Brian shut down against pain so automatically that all awareness of anything disturbing was blocked. He couldn't recognize the pain of his children, for to do so would have raised the possibility that he would feel his own. Yet, most of the time, Brian appeared to be warm and available. Peter, by contrast, was more overtly shut down, unavailable for any interaction most of the time.

In contrast to their spouses, Brian's sister, Julie, and his wife, Kathy, developed false hope to defend themselves against the painful reality of their childhoods. Julie's false hope centered on the belief that enough distress on her part could evoke a caring response from her parents. Although in reality that maneuver failed, the effort behind it was unconscious, so the defeat went unrecognized and the unreal hope continued. She married a man who behaved in ways that put her in an unattended-to position similar to the one she had experienced as a child. This enabled her to keep attempting to change her parents symbolically, through interaction with her distant husband. Her struggle with him ranged from tears to tirades. Kathy's false hope led her to choose a man whose unconscious need was to be given attention, so she could continue the old attempt to get the love she needed as a child—from a man who was really needy and self-centered.

It is interesting to note, and important to realize, that although in most cases the person chosen as a symbol will show personality traits very similar to those of the parent about whom the struggle (or the need to withdraw) originated, sometimes the person will not. Brian appeared to be emotionally available, while Peter's absence was unmistakable. Julie showed her neediness and displeasure quite readily, while Kathy's were hidden in her caretaking behavior.

IDENTIFYING OUR SYMBOLS

In order to cultivate healthy relationships, we must develop an ability to discern which people are symbols for us. Fortunately, whether the traits are obvious or hidden, this can be done; but unfortunately, like Brian, Kathy, Peter, and Julie, most people unknowingly live their adult lives as if they were still in childhood. Whatever we are still unconsciously "working on" getting, or protecting ourselves from—that is, an old, unmet need from childhood—will actively affect our thoughts, feelings, and behavior in the most important areas of our lives.

Our cultural child-rearing methods have been determined by what Alice Miller calls "poisonous pedagogy," a philosophy that sees the human infant and small child as innately selfish and abusive to others and therefore in need of being "taught," often in physically and emotionally ruthless ways, to be unselfish and caring. The absurdity of this thinking is thoroughly addressed in Miller's *For Your Own Good* and *Thou Shalt Not Be Aware*. Because of these cultural patterns, which sanction rather than inhibit many forms of child abuse and neglect, it would be a rare adult who is not the unconscious carrier of some repressed childhood pain and truth. Thus most people are unconsciously relating to some aspects of their lives from the perspective of the children they were instead of the adults they are. These aspects are always central to our lives, and when we are "children" in relation to them, they are "symbols" for us.

If you want to do the healing work, recognizing your basic

tendency—whether you struggle with people and situations, or avoid them through shutting down—will help you determine just who or what in your adult life is a symbol for you. It is in our symbolic relationships that we feel and act like the children we were, and while those symbols are often people, they can also be such things as where we live, what we do for a living, and even the car we want to own or the clothes we want to buy. For the overreactor, the person or situation with whom she is struggling—attempting to change without success—is a symbol. For the underreactor, the person who is important to him, but with whom he does not want to "open up," is a symbol. Sometimes avoiders try to lead solitary lives, and are attracted to self-isolating jobs like sheepherding, cow punching, or manning forest-fire lookouts; or they may find themselves in professions like accounting or forms of scientific research that involve data more than people. Clothes and cars can also be symbolic in that they tend to be used to communicate to others something about the individual wearing or driving them. Some people may make these choices consciously to help achieve specific effects; but others may not. A common unconscious use for items like clothes and cars is to try to please a parent (even if dead) by maintaining a certain appearance in public that is not necessarily consistent with our real selves. Such an unconscious influence can make us dress and drive either "better" than we would otherwise or "worse," depending on our individual histories.

OBJECTIVE SELF-OBSERVATION

Identifying the symbols in your life brings you closer to being able to stop living in the past, controlled by unconscious drives. With your symbols identified, you are in a position to begin developing the skill of objective self-observation, which is necessary in order to be able to make conscious choices about what you will *do* in any given situation, no matter what you may be *feeling*.

"Objective" does not mean that you don't have strong feelings; rather, it means that you learn to separate your rational thought process from the emotional part of yourself in order to *watch* what is happening to you internally. In a sense, you "contain" the feelings where they exist physically—in the heart, chest, stomach, or intestines—while you examine the situation mentally. This *does not* mean that you don't experience feelings. It *does* mean that you don't allow them to influence your thinking or dictate your behavior.

Situations that occur without warning, such as what happened to Joan when she saw that the snow had smashed her windshield and felt that she had to run to George to be told what to do, can also be symbols. In such cases, there is no ongoing struggle or avoidance in relation to a person who is a symbol, but you can learn to identify the kinds of events that tend to shift you suddenly into your childhood state of consciousness. For Joan, the clue is that she felt she had to be told what to do, which means that she felt "little." This feeling is unlikely to be unique to this one situation. Other examples of the same phenomenon might be, for instance, being very uncomfortable going to a movie by yourself because you're sure everyone is looking at you and thinking that no one wants to be with you; or being insecure about wearing the "right thing" at social gatherings; or feeling excessively "stupid" when you are unable to recall an acquaintance's name; or obsessing for hours about a conversation in which you feel you could have expressed yourself better. Pay close attention to anything that consistently makes you feel like the small child you once were. This takes some practice. Learning to do what is necessary for healing work involves concentration and practice in much the same way as learning a physical activity such as skiing does.

MONITORING YOUR RESPONSE

Many people have become so accustomed either to completely "skipping" their feelings and moving automatically into thinking, or to allowing their feelings to influence their thinking, that it takes a good deal of time and effort to change those habits. The first challenge, then, may be to become aware of the separate functions of your emotional responses: what happens in your body when you feel; whether you can think separately (objectively) from your feelings; whether you think instead of feel; or whether you think based on your feelings.

This exercise takes a certain amount of self-discipline, since the unconscious drive that makes us struggle with someone or avoid feelings also makes us feel as if we *must* respond as we do. For example, when Julie badgers Peter to be more emotionally open and physically available to her and the children, he reacts by withdrawing further, telling Julie that she expects too much, or becoming angry and stalking out. If Peter were doing this healing work, it would be precisely at the moment he wants to withdraw that he would need to observe himself dispassionately. He would have to try to notice that he is feeling threatened and wants to defend himself. It would be OK for Peter to leave, but he would need to develop enough self-control to try to connect with what he is feeling rather than simply shutting down as usual. In other words, to be truly objective, Peter has to begin to look at what is happening inside himself that drives him to behave in this way.

Brian, whose avoidance of feelings is covert, has to find a way to realize when he is shutting down, since he does nothing obvious. His children's complaints could be a clue to him that he is avoiding something and may provide an opportunity for him to take the time to look at what he might be feeling (after the children's needs are responded to). It is even more likely that Brian's feelings will surface if it is Kathy who leaves him to attend to the children, since, as a symbol, she is *abandoning* him.

As a struggler doing the healing work, Julie would have to set aside her strong conviction of how important it is to her and the children for Peter to change. When she finds herself beginning to cry or scold, she will have to step back deliberately from what feels like a very powerful present need, in order to practice separating her feelings from her rational abilities, and observe the pattern of her interactions.

MAKING CONSCIOUS CHOICES

This process reminds me of some lessons I once took to learn to play a particular game of poker. One of the lessons involved folding (throwing in the hand) no matter how good the prospect of winning. When confronted with how difficult it was to fold with three aces, I realized that the lesson was intended to reduce the extent to which I might be emotionally attached to the outcome of any particular hand. It would increase my tolerance for short-term losses so I would be less vulnerable to fear, which leads to bad judgment. In other words, I would have more control over my decision-making ability.

To consciously choose to behave differently from the way you feel compelled to behave is essential for this work to be successful, and it is very difficult. The compulsion to continue to do whatever you usually do is quite powerful—and the conscious mind will find reasons why it is OK to continue. It is common to feel an urgency that can override whatever good intentions you have.

In spite of the difficulty, the ability to detach from emotions and to respond on the basis of conscious choice must be developed in order to do this healing work. When couples such as Brian and Kathy or Julie and Peter are doing regressive work, the power of the process is enhanced, since they are each other's symbols. Once they are able to recognize their defenses and are willing to feel the old pain that is being brought up, they can respond in a supportive way to each other. In intimate relationships, each person is almost always a symbol to the other in a way that perfectly matches the repressed needs of their childhoods, as we have seen. When both partners are willing to work on overcoming the effects of their histories, the customary hurt feelings, arguments, misunderstandings, disappointments, and anger stop causing misery and confusion and lead instead to healing and healthy interaction. Ultimately, this process can break the generational cycle of family dysfunction.

chapter seven

The Art of
Self-Observation:
Taking a Step Toward
Authentic Adult Life

We have seen how our defenses against the pain of childhood experiences result in our unconscious selection of love partners who are symbolic for our parent(s), and from whom we try to get the unmet needs of the children we were satisfied. We have seen, too, that our unconscious controls our adult choices in many important ways, affecting not only the type of people with whom we fall in love but other aspects of our lives as well. As the prime concern for most of us is to have a satisfying, fulfilling love relationship, we will focus now on that concern in describing how to overcome these unconscious influences.

A CRUCIAL POINT

The interactions between Brian and Kathy and Julie and Peter reveal that each related toward his or her partner out of their childhood defense of either unreal hope or emotional shutdown. As we have seen, there was a point in their interactions at which each had an opportunity to interrupt her or his defensive behavior pattern. This is extremely important: for all of us, the ability to recognize this moment depends on objective self-observation; without it, we will continue to be swept up in the emotion involved and, in the old way of interacting, without being at all aware of what we are dong. Once that crucial point is recognized, however, we are in a position to respond in a different way. This new response is part of the healing process. Objective self-observation is not an effort to *feel* differently—changes in the way we feel come later. Rather, it is an effort to respond in a new way, *despite* the way we feel. But there are two powerful impediments to our being able to do this: the strength of the emotional state we are in when involved in a symbolic encounter, and fear. We will discuss the former first.

THE PULL OF THE CHILDHOOD STATE

Typical reactions to people who are symbols in our lives include arguing, badgering, criticizing, complaining, whining, blaming, yelling, seething, withdrawing, refusing to talk, denying there's anything wrong, and retaliating, to name but a few. All of these behaviors are indications that we are feeling emotional distress. Of course, we are not always engaging in an old, childhood response when we feel emotional distress; we all have many present experiences that range from unpleasant to extremely painful. However, if we are arguing, badgering, blaming, etc., then we are not dealing with the way we feel in a conscious, responsible manner. Many times we may temporarily respond to a person or situation in these dysfunctional ways and then, realizing what we are doing, correct ourselves. When we are able to do so, it is likely that whatever is happening is simply a present event and not a symbolic "trigger." The bona fide clue that we are caught up in the old childhood response is that we either continue to press the situation, despite repeated failure, or we continue to try to escape it with no success, still believing that we can. We are unable to recognize that our actions are not producing the results we want, and so we cannot change them. At times like this, our unconscious is in charge.

We have all known couples like Sally and Dan who habitually

and publicly argue about staying or leaving a party or accuse one another of drinking, flirting, or talking too much at social events. The confrontation is sometimes blatant, sometimes subtle, but it happens every time. They never seem to go home, figure out how to settle the difference, and then take care of it. Similarly, most of us have had a friend like Lisa who periodically calls to complain about her boyfriend Martin's roving eye, asks for advice on how to handle it, and commits herself to acting on the advice—only to call again sometime later with exactly the same problem. At that point, Lisa says that she had believed that Martin had mended his ways and so she had "backed off." Now she knows that this was a mistake, she says; this time she's going to do what's effective. But she continues to go on and on.

We ourselves might be quietly tolerating the loneliness of a relationship with someone either physically or emotionally absent most of the time. Or perhaps we find ourselves the continual target of undeserved irritability—all the while attempting to be cheerful, pleasing company and thinking our efforts will produce changes that somehow never happen. Yet we go on thinking of new ways to act that might "work."

We can reverse this unconsciously motivated process and gain control by stopping the behavior as soon as we realize what we are doing and focusing on the feeling instead. In order to do this, we must be willing to let go of the current interaction, at least for the time being. This is not easy to do, since the "heat of the moment" makes it difficult to drop; but unless we can learn to do this, self-observation cannot happen.

The process of observing your feelings takes the place of whatever emotionally loaded reaction is usual for you. Even withdrawal, as silent as it may be, is a behavior that is full of feeling—albeit denied. Likewise, the most open and volatile struggles may also indicate the presence of denied feelings, for the actual pain that is at the heart of such behavior is hidden from the persons engaged. By definition, the emotionally painful feelings that are denied but are behind the struggling or withdrawal are the childhood pain that was never fully experienced consciously. This is why healing cannot occur without an interruption of the defensive behavior.

I am not suggesting that you interrupt established patterns in order to make your behavior more "functional," as do many therapists, who seem to aim at changing behavior as an end in itself. People described as "co-dependent" are encouraged to become familiar with the things they do that are "co-dependent behaviors" and then consciously act in a different manner. Those who are successful in doing this are considered to be "in recovery," yet many complain that they continue to find themselves in destructive relationships or feel "depressed."

The process I advocate here is not an end but a *means* to an end. We are revisiting our childhood pain and allowing ourselves to feel its full impact so we will no longer have past-based secrets from ourselves and the consequent need to misperceive reality in order to hide from unconscious pain.

Once you have learned to recognize your repetitive patterns of either struggling or avoiding, you must make a conscious effort to disrupt these entrenched reactions and try to observe what you are feeling instead. I say "try to," because many of you will not be in touch with any feelings at all, while others will be feeling intensely but *not* the emotions that underlie what appears to be happening. This effort will take time. If you are the type to struggle with your partner, it is best to remove yourself physically for this observation. On the other hand, if it is your habit to withdraw, engaging in interaction, attempting to communicate what you may be feeling, and then continuing to reflect on your emotions by yourself will help you overcome your defenses. In other words, defenses are most quickly broken by doing the *opposite* of what you want to do at the time.

For Brian, this meant that he had to break the pattern of sending the children away when they interrupted his quiet time with Kathy. As part of doing this work, he and Kathy agreed that when Kathy left to meet the children's needs, Brian would go into another room by himself. The first time he did so, he found that he was feeling angry. Prior to beginning this healing work, without his ever becoming aware of it, Brian would have directed that anger at his children; but he now saw that his anger was not really caused by them. In order to use this "time out" opportunity to practice observing his feelings instead of reacting to them, he just sat there, experiencing the anger and noting how it felt in his body. After doing this a number of times, Brian began to be aware of another feeling under the anger. As he relaxed and opened up to this new feeling, the anger disappeared, and he found himself beginning to feel very sad, with tears coming to his eyes. Brian was surprised, for he had not felt sad in a long time. In fact, he only vaguely remembered feeling sad as a child. This was as far as he could take this feeling for some time.

For Julie, the effort to begin her healing work meant that she had to disengage instead of pursue a struggle with Peter. She had the opportunity to try this one day when she wanted Peter to go on a picnic with her and the kids and Peter refused, saying he didn't want to leave the football game that was on television. At first, Julie felt angry and hurt and became tearful, telling Peter how little she felt he cared about her and the children. It seemed to her that some silly game was always more important. Julie recognized then that she was struggling with Peter, but her mind told her that surely anyone would feel the way she did in this situation, whether they had childhood issues or not. Still, Julie mustered all her strength and was able to turn away from the situation, ignoring her desire to continue. She went into their bedroom, lay on the bed, and began to cry. While crying, she observed that she was feeling totally left out, ignored, unimportant, and lonely. She let herself feel how that loneliness felt in her body. It hurt in her chest as she cried.

Both Brian and Julie made conscious contact with the feelings that underlay unsatisfactory relationship interactions in which they had found themselves many times. To accomplish this, it was first necessary for them to practice self-observation and recognize the point at which they would usually revert to defensive behavior. They then exercised the self-control needed to disengage from the interaction and *do something different than they had desired.* They were able to go to a quiet place and, focusing inward, allow themselves to feel and recognize their repressed emotions.

The difficulty in making the choice to behave differently from the way you feel compelled to behave cannot be overstated. The urgency you experience at the time comes from the unconscious mind's belief that your life is in danger (a result of your having shifted into your childhood state of consciousness). The power of this state can easily override whatever intentions you have to put this process into action. It is only later, after regaining emotional equilibrium (shifting back to your adult state), that you will see, in hindsight, that you missed the moment. More experience with this phenomenon along with continued self-observation will bring you to the point where you begin to "catch" the true meaning of what is happening and respond in a corrective way despite the strength of this pull.

DEALING WITH FEAR

A second impediment, *fear,* must also be overcome. At some point in the process, usually after you have successfully begun to drop your defensive maneuvers, you may be gripped with anxiety ranging from apprehension to terror. The reason is that the defenses you are dropping are those that protected you from painful emotions that could have killed you as a child. In your unconscious, these feelings are "coded" as life-threatening; therefore fear is always felt as part of this process. The unconscious creates the fear to discourage you from going farther into the experience, as it "believes" you can be damaged.

The fear will feel very real. This, too, is due to the shift in consciousness back into childhood reality, so that what was true then, but not acknowledged, feels true now. In effect, people experiencing this *are* back in childhood emotionally—but not physically, geographically, or in time. What makes fighting the fear even more difficult is that the conscious mind gives us present-day "reasons" for being afraid.

For example, when alone at night, secure in their own houses, doors and windows locked, some people will believe that they have overlooked a point of access or fear that an intruder somehow got in earlier and is hiding; typically, even if they check all the rooms, the closets, and under all the beds, they will still think it possible that the intruder was shifting his hiding place, keeping one step ahead or behind them, still present and a menace. Others, walking at night down the street of a small town where everyone knows everyone else, rationalize their fear by clinging to the slim possibility that someone "crazed" could be behind the next tree, having been lured by the attraction of a small, sleepy, unguarded town. (Yes, it's possible, but so, theoretically, is winning the lottery.) There are other, social rationalizations that seem to be "good" reasons for fear—someone will hear about what you did or said and ostracize you; you will be "hated." Perhaps your fear is simply that you may be "yelled at"—something that can really hurt a child but not an adult. On later examination, reasoning such as this proves false, but at the time, because of the consciousness shift, it seems very valid.

That our whole culture accepts certain childhood realities as true of adult life affects this situation as well (see Chapter Three). When we believe that the loss of a love relationship can devastate us, and that this reaction is normal for adults—and the belief is fostered by books, movies, songs, and friends—then taking any action that would threaten the relationship can be overwhelmingly frightening, even if action is necessary for our own well-being. But this belief is actually a culturally accepted unconscious projection of a childhood truth (abandonment) onto adult life. If we continue to accept it as adult truth, then we will respond to our feelings of fear in a protective manner and be unable to drop our defenses.

Emotional trauma that we were unable to experience was once a threat to our physical survival, so when we act in ways that allow the unfelt feelings to surface, we will feel an amount of fear commensurate with an actual life-threatening situation. The ability you have developed to observe yourself can be used to get through this. As soon as you recognize how afraid you feel, take a moment to look around and ask yourself whether anything is threatening your *physical* safety. If the answer is no, then proceed with the process, refusing to act in accordance with your fears. People often say at this point, "But it *feels* like my safety is actually at risk." This is, of course, because, at this moment, they are in their childhood state of consciousness, which means that *everything* feels as if it's *then*. You have to experience this enough times to begin to see, in retrospect, that there is actually nothing to fear. At some point, you will be able to "act against the fear," further opening the way to feeling your repressed childhood pain.

The phenomenon of fear can actually be useful, since it can lead you into feeling the pain of repressed experiences (which in turn makes grieving, and thus healing, possible). However, it is often difficult to know exactly how to "do the right thing," especially when you are gripped by strong emotions. Fortunately, fear can be used to help you find out, because it will attempt to lead you *away from* whatever can help the recovery process the most. Remember, since fear is attempting to protect you from something that needs to be felt, you should simply *act against the fear*—that is, do whatever it is "telling" you not to do (or refrain from doing whatever it is telling you to do). When you have checked the particular circumstance and have found that no true physical (or financial) danger is present, *do whatever you are afraid to do*. This internally generated fear is like a signpost directing you, but it takes courage to follow it. Spending some time after the fact evaluating whether you really could have been "hurt" can help develop the courage you need.

TAKING STEPS TOWARD HEALING

Each person needs to grapple successfully with these situations and overcome the strong emotional pull and the fear in order to participate in the healing process.

Julie, for instance, had to overcome the temptation to stay in the struggle with Peter. It took effort to turn away from that, since she clearly *wanted* to keep after him with her complaints. Her successful move away from this did not come easily; there were many previous occasions when she couldn't stop herself. It was almost impossible for Julie to see how "giving up on Peter" (which is what it felt like)

could help anything: yes, she told herself, Peter is like her father in
some ways, and she didn't get what she needed from her father, but
how would it help her to let Peter "off the hook" now? Wasn't that
what assertiveness was all about, she wondered—deciding what you
want and not settling for anything less?

For people who struggle to change someone, this way of thinking will be very familiar. However, it ignores the fact that continuing to struggle with Peter will never get Julie what she thinks she
wants as an adult. All it will do is keep alive her unconscious hope
of getting love from a shut-down man (her father). *It is not Peter
she needs to give up on, it is the struggle.*

When Julie came to understand this better, she had the will to
assert herself in a truly healthy way—against the arguments her
mind offered her to keep struggling, and against her own desire to
do so. It was this awareness and willingness that led Julie to be able
to leave the living room on that weekend football day and begin to
connect with her old pain.

During this first connecting experience, as she lay on the bed
crying and feeling the pain in her chest, Julie became afraid. She
was surprised by the fact that the experience actually *hurt* and
feared that she might somehow be damaging something in her body.
However, because she had been told that overcoming fear is part of
the process, and that emotional pain really does hurt physically, she
"screwed up her courage" and continued to "go into" the feeling. As
she cried and felt more and more like the child she once was, Julie
realized that it was actually the feeling of being so alone and
uncared for that was frightening to her—that this was *part* of the old
experience and simply needed to be accepted. After a while, Julie
found that the tears seemed to dry up, and the painful feelings left
her. She felt tired, but oddly peaceful. The beauty of the sunny af-
ternoon again attracted her. She got up, blew her nose, packed a
lunch, called to the children, and left with them for a picnic. They
had fun and, for the time being, Julie couldn't have cared less what
Peter was doing.

The previous illustration circumvents certain life realities that
will sooner or later have to be taken into account. Julie and Peter

have children, so there will naturally be times when Julie will not have the luxury of simply going into the bedroom, lying down, and feeling her pain.

When something happens to trigger repressed childhood feelings and you are in a situation that prevents you from taking the time to go into them, you will have to use even more effort not to be controlled by your defenses. If you are at work, you can sometimes excuse yourself, go into the restroom, and cry—providing you are not loud and your retreat is short-lived. But when this is neither adequate nor practical, or when you are at home and the children need you, the regressive feeling work has to be postponed.

In these instances it will most likely be very difficult to control your defenses, but you must make the effort. If you are successful, you have the opportunity to contain the emotion within your body while you finish the task at hand. It may be helpful to visualize a little basket, carried in your abdomen or stomach, holding the feeling. In a sense, you are "saving it" for later by consciously continuing to feel the discomfort where it is in your body while, on the outside, you are behaving normally. Then, when the appropriate time comes, you can do as Julie did. This is not "stuffing it." "Stuffing it" implies suppression, a conscious effort to avoid the feeling.

As you can see, it is necessary to overcome what seems to be your own desire in the moment, as well as the fear that follows when you begin to break down your defenses, in order to access the childhood pain underlying struggle or avoidance. Connecting with the painful emotions that were previously hidden by defensive behavior opens the door to the grieving that was never done but can be done now. These initial grief experiences offer a glimpse of the adult state of being (which emerges briefly) and a taste of what it is like to be free of unconscious interference. As your grieving work continues and you spend more and more time in the authentic adult state, you can expect these good feelings to become increasingly familiar.

chapter eight

The Powerful
Process of Grieving

When Brian and Julie allowed themselves to feel the pain that they had been carrying but were unable to acknowledge due to their defenses, they felt the emotional impact of the abuse they had experienced growing up in their families. As children, it had been necessary for them to protect themselves from this impact by repressing, or blocking it out.

It bears repeating that, although it is safe for us to feel these painful emotions now that we are adults, it will not *feel* safe due to the influence of the unconscious. In fact, it will feel as dangerous as it actually would have been in childhood. When we stop engaging in defensive behavior, the block can be removed, enabling us to feel the pain that was once so dangerous. But when we do remove the block we experience pain *exactly the way we would have felt it then*, including the fear of feeling it.

When we become defensive in relation to our symbols, a shift into the childhood state of consciousness has occurred. That is where our defenses originated. When we are struggling with or avoiding something, we are *always* in our childhood state of consciousness. If we are not aware of this (as is the case with most people, who have no information about this), then we continue to "act out of the childhood state"—something that never has good results. Once we recognize that this shift has occurred—and our defensive behavior is the clue—we can try to stop the action, remove ourselves, and focus inward; if we do so successfully, we will feel what happened in childhood in its pure form, unaffected by anything that has happened since the original abusive event that caused the feelings to be blocked.

Remember, the unconscious represses the feelings *before* they can be felt. They have therefore *never* been truly experienced until now, when they emerge as if in response to a present event. These feelings are not available to us when we sit and talk about our childhoods and remember with our conscious minds. It is *only* the emotion of the moment, which is brought up through interaction with our symbols, that allows us to enter our unconscious memories. In doing so, we "go back" emotionally to the time before the block. This process gives us another chance to live through what happened then—but now, when we have the strength to do it.

LIVING A MEMORY

In order to "live a memory now," we have to:

1. Give up any effort to control the experience;
2. Consciously agree to feel whatever is happening;
3. "Go with" the experience as totally as possible.

Complete openness at this time will lead to the recovery of memories previously unrecognized at a conscious level because of repression, but the fear that almost always accompanies these regressive experiences makes such surrender difficult.

In the last chapter we discussed the need to respond to this fear first by checking external reality to make sure that no actual dangers—physical or financial—exist. Although the fear comes from our unconscious, as do the feelings we are attempting to feel, it is our conscious, rational abilities that help us during this part of the process. Because our conscious mind functions in the present, adult reality, it is the part of the mind we use to find out whether any real danger exists. Once we are sure there is no present threat to our safety, we continue to use the rational part of our mind to overcome the effects of this fear.

It is likely that throughout your adult life you have shifted back and forth between present and past reality—between childhood and adulthood. In fact, it is possible that you have spent more time in your childhood reality than you have in your adult state. (Some people have reported that they had *never* been in a total, authentic adult state before they began to do this work.) Unfortunately, however, these shifts have occurred without any awareness on your part.

As you practice self-observation and begin to understand these concepts, you should also start to recognize these changes in consciousness. When you become aware that you are suddenly feeling like the child you were in your family of origin, a shift has taken place. But the fact that you can observe this happening also means that you are, or can be, aware that you are not actually back there. This capacity—to *feel* as if you're in childhood, while *knowing* you actually are not—enables you to maintain a certain equilibrium despite the fears and other distressing feelings assaulting you. Again, it is not that you don't feel them, because it is important that you do. At the same time, however, part of your mind (the conscious, present-day part) knows that there is nothing happening now to warrant the distressful feelings and that there is no need to *do* anything except feel them.

LEARNING TO GRIEVE

Let's take a look at how underreactors and overreactors typically work through such moments. As you may remember, Brian, Kathy's husband, tended to underreact to triggering situations. At home, he had to learn to overcome his tendency to withdraw instead of admitting to himself that he felt hurt and angry. He had to learn to move toward that which he was unconsciously motivated to move away from.

As he continued with regression work, something similar happened to him at work. Brian's job paid well, which was important to him and his family, and he enjoyed the work itself, which included making frequent business trips away from the office; but his immediate supervisors were unethical people who maneuvered dishonestly in business dealings and cheated their staff financially whenever possible. When it was necessary for Brian to confront one of them about something, he always found himself being "stone-walled" and outmaneuvered. Before beginning regression work, Brian typically rationalized the actions of his employers, shrugging his shoulders and making light of them. Deciding it "wasn't important," he would drop his need for clarification of the situation and simply make some adaptation. In his conversations with Kathy, he reported these incidents quite casually, while Kathy's response was usually more intense. This often led to arguments, since Brian had a stake in minimizing these issues. He did not want to deal with them or, more important, with the feelings they engendered in him. However, Kathy's confrontations forced Brian to admit how bad his employers' actions made him feel, and since these things continued to occur he began to feel emotionally distressed while at work.

Brian then came to see that he needed to use the same process he was engaged in at home with regard to the way these employers were making him feel. He knew that his discomfort was reality-based, but he also knew that the job was bringing up the childhood feelings of his needs being ignored and his life being controlled by his parents. One element uniting past and present was that, in both cases, Brian could do nothing about the problem. He was not even in a position to leave for another job, at least in the foreseeable future, since this one paid better than anything else available in his small town.

It was not feasible for Brian to "move into" the situation at work as he did at home, opening up verbally about how he felt, since that could threaten his employment. In this case, being willing to admit the seriousness of these actions and the effect they had on him enabled Brian to begin to feel the pain associated with the childhood events to which they were connected.

Brian arranged for some time alone when he got home at the end of the workday. He would sit quietly or lie down, and mentally "see himself" back at the office that day. Visualizing his employer, he realized what he would really have liked to say to him and began to talk to him, out loud. It took some effort for Brian to even begin to know what he wanted to say, because he was accustomed to overlooking those feelings. He began haltingly and had to pause to consider each statement. Gradually, the words came faster and more easily, eventually flowing out more and more loudly until Brian was shouting in rage, pounding his fist. Suddenly the rage became a rush of tears and he experienced an engulfing feeling of sadness and loss in the area of his heart. Brian found himself weeping like the lost little boy he had been, helpless to change what had obviously been so wrong. Although Brian felt drained after his tears subsided, he also had new realizations about how things had been for him as a child.

Following several similar episodes, Brian was able to recognize his feelings at work as they happened and to admit the ugly reality of how his workplace was run, but he was largely free of the intense distress, connected to childhood events, that had accompanied this recognition. When the old feelings occasionally came up, it was clear to him that it was not his employers' actions that had enough power over him to cause those feelings. Although he was no longer minimizing (underreacting) the situation, he also knew that he did not need to take any present action; rather, what would be effective was his letting himself feel the truth of the past. Of course, he would continue to keep checking the job market for a better place to work that paid as well.

To illustrate this same process with someone who typically overreacted, we can look at Ida, who grew up with a father who had an explosive temper. He never hit anyone, but he would yell and swear and throw things around when frustrated. Ida's husband, Hank, was the same way. Ida felt terrified whenever Hank lost his temper because it brought up her feelings from childhood, but she also found her fear puzzling because she remembered simply going to her room to play during her father's outbursts and had the impression that they didn't really bother her. The intense fear she felt when Hank exploded was the feeling she had defended herself against in the past.

After learning to observe herself with some objectivity, Ida began to be able to assess the present situation rationally even while she was feeling terrified. The first time she was completely successful was one day when she and Hank were traveling and came out of a restaurant after having lunch to find that their car had a flat tire. Hank blew up, swearing at the car, kicking the tire, slamming the jack to the ground, and so forth. Ida observed how fearful she felt, letting herself experience the intensity of sensation in her stomach and chest and the way her breathing came fast and shallow. She also paid attention to what was really happening—yes, Hank was yelling and throwing things around, but there was no actual danger to her. She could see that Hank had no intention of hurting her, and she knew from experience that he had never hurt her. It was clear, then, that her fear came from her experiences with her father. He had never hurt anyone physically either, but since a small child cannot make deductions about what to expect based on past experiences, the terror of what he *might* do would still have been part of the experience had she not repressed it. Now, however, the knowledge that the fear was "old" and that no real, present danger existed enabled Ida to stand there, watch and listen to her husband, and let herself feel like the small child she had been during her father's tantrums. Soon tears were coursing down her cheeks as she surrendered to feeling the child's fear.*

---

*This phrase—"the child's fear"—may sound awkward. We are more accustomed to referring to "a child," or (more recently in some current literature) "my child." I use different wording for specific reasons. "The child" is accurate because, when our consciousness shifts into our childhood state, it is the reality of our own childhood to which we return. "A child" would imply that everyone's childhood feels the same, which is not true. We may all share similarities, but the events and painful feelings attached to them are our own, and different from anyone else's.

"*My* child" is not accurate for a number of reasons. Obviously, we are adults regardless of what our state of consciousness is. The idea that we "have a child inside" (the source of the term

When Ida allowed herself to be affected by the pain of her childhood experiences with her rageful father and spontaneously started crying, she was beginning the grief process. She consciously chose to admit that Hank's temper display was a symbol for her, since the fear she felt had no present reality base. She had been with Hank long enough to know that she would not be physically hurt by him, or even emotionally assaulted through name-calling, blaming, or other verbal abuse. Ida was able to give in to feelings that belonged in the childhood she had spent with a rageful father. The child she was could not have had the capacity to figure out that Daddy's blowups were not physically dangerous to her—and they *were* emotionally dangerous. Unlike the adult Ida became, she could not, as a child, have chosen to leave her family. In addition, she *needed* her father to be a person capable of loving her enough to meet her need for feeling safe and secure. His temper made this impossible, and for Ida to have allowed herself to recognize that would have threatened her survival. Beneath this was an even deeper fear—the terror of admitting the truth of her father's incapacity *ever* to meet her need for security. When Hank exploded over the flat tire, Ida's acceptance while in her childhood state that it was neces-

---

"my child") was meant to be a metaphor for this childhood state of consciousness, but many have taken the expression literally. Some therapists have even expanded on this idea, and not only talk about "your child" but base their treatment programs on helping you to nurture this child, giving to it now, from "your adult," what it didn't get then. This is not only a mistake but dangerous, since it fragments us into pieces of selves—and some people are already using fragmentation as a defense. What is needed is more integration, not more separation.

In any event, this way of thinking is just plain nonsensical. We don't "have" a child in the first place. And if we did, we couldn't make the past any different by doing things now. Even if we recognize the terminology as the metaphor it is, when we feel ourselves to be in that childhood state we may still think we can heal the old hurts by giving ourselves the loving we didn't get then. Some therapists encourage individual regression to an infant state in a group setting, then prompt the group to "welcome the child" into the world with loving words. This may temporarily feel very good, but it cannot heal. We are not now the baby we were, and it is *only* that baby who needed to be welcomed lovingly into the world. The adults we have actually become no longer need this. When we are in that early state of consciousness, we may think or feel that we need it (perhaps in some symbolic form), but it is *not possible* to return to that time and satisfy that need. The event in question is over and done. What is not over and done is the memory of, or pain connected to, the event. While we cannot *correct it* through regression, we can return *to know and feel it*. This is the only way healing can take place. Since it is "the child we were" who has to know what happened and feel the pain of it, I use "the child" to refer to the state of consciousness in which the old pain is felt.

sary to open to the fear instead of running from it set her on the path to realizing this underlying truth and feeling her grief.

RELEASING AND HEALING BURIED FEELINGS

Our childhood pain is usually felt in "layers" similar to Ida's, although arranged according to our own unique histories. Once the fear is allowed to be in our bodies, accepted for what it is (old but real fear of feeling dangerous emotional pain or truth about something), and lived with for a time, the feeling will "drop into" another layer. Under the fear, other deeply painful feelings—sadness, loss, abandonment, hopelessness, pain of ridicule, rage, shame, not being wanted, etc.—are found, the specific feelings depending on our personal history.

Many of us have hoped to change these things through traditional therapy, but insight alone can never change unconsciously based feelings. Fear is one of the most uncomfortable, since it cannot be "cried out." It is understandable that we all want the realizations that can be gained in traditional, insight-oriented therapy, or the emotional release that is being encouraged by some of the newer therapies to relieve us from our fears, but this is not enough. Further, fear, like any other feeling, has to be allowed to process within our systems. It will "work itself through" if we simply accept that we must feel it, carry it around with us—doing nothing to attempt to make it go away—while we go about our daily business.

"Living with the fear" (or any other painful feeling) simply means letting the discomfort remain in your body, without trying to get rid of it. This is very hard to do; we have spent our lives automatically attempting to protect ourselves. Changing to unconditional acceptance will take time and effort. It means being willing to maintain almost constant vigilance over what you are feeling and allowing it to happen to you, day after day, hour after hour. Surrendering to something you have always unconsciously believed could kill you is something that can be done only little by little. It will take both time and energy. (Because this process involves emotional and mental effort, most people are surprised at how tired they become when engaging in it. It is important to realize this and allow extra time in your daily schedule to accommodate what will probably be an increased need for rest and sleep.)

The tears that first came when Ida gave in to the need simply to let her fear affect her (while recognizing it as old) soon ended, but an uncomfortable, anxious feeling remained. She said nothing to Hank, who had been so engrossed in his tire problem that he hadn't noticed. They went on their way, with Ida showing none of her feelings, except for perhaps being quieter than usual. Hank *did* notice that Ida was not behaving as usual—hurt and critical, expecting an apology—following such an experience with him. Ida's quietness meant that she was dealing with her feelings where they truly belonged—in the past. Hank's behavior had only triggered them for her symbolically.

Ida would deal with the issue of whether she wanted to continue in a relationship with someone so rageful and out of control later, when her childhood had been substantially grieved and she was no longer so influenced by feeling like the child she had been; adult decisions cannot be made effectively when the childhood state of consciousness is so dominant. For the next several hours, Ida let her fear affect her internally, while externally she went about her business. The next day she suddenly realized the fear was gone.

Each time Ida experienced this fear, whatever the ostensible cause, she first mentally checked her environment to make sure that there was nothing of present physical or financial danger to her, and then she let it take hold of her as before. She found that the feelings of fear became weaker and weaker. Ida also found, however, that she began to feel other painful emotions, the first of which was loneliness. It was natural for her to explain this feeling in terms of the time Hank spent watching sports on TV or hunting with his buddies. She began to struggle with him, telling him he should stay home more and implying something was wrong with their relationship since he didn't want to spend more time with her. This escalated into Ida's pushing Hank to talk more, to share his feelings with her. She felt deprived not only of companionship but of emotional intimacy. In the past, Ida had felt a certain relief at the distance

Hank kept from her, as a buffer against his outbursts. It made her feel safer. Now that she was less fearful, she began to want more from him. After several weeks of attempting to get his attention by making nice dinners, planning activities, or scolding him— sometimes with anger, sometimes with tears—for his failure to be closer, Ida suddenly realized that she was struggling and that she was probably being motivated by old, unconscious needs.

It was time for Ida to apply the same methods in dealing with her feeling of loneliness as she had in response to her fear. Hank was surprised and relieved when Ida stopped hassling him but, as was his way, said nothing. Internally, Ida started to feel how painful loneliness was. As she allowed that pain to be present in her body, she began to be aware that it felt more like "being alone" than lone- liness. The painful feeling became more localized until it was a con- stant ache in the area of her stomach. Most of the time, she took care of daily chores as usual, but sometimes the ache became so strong that she let herself stop so she could respond to the feeling.

She would lie on her bed, focusing on the ache, and let herself ponder her life, slowly reviewing the times she had felt this feeling before. Ida made a conscious effort to look only for the feeling itself rather than try to figure out what might be causing it. She recalled having had that same ache in her stomach many times, and kept moving backward in her memory until she finally "saw" herself, alone in her bedroom, at about five years of age. She was playing with her dolls, pretending not to hear her father shouting and her mother crying in the other room. When this memory returned, Ida let herself feel like the five-year-old she had been, mentally putting herself into the picture she had seen. She let herself hear the shout- ing and the crying and feel the pain she had been feeling for days, but *this* time it was connected to that childhood event. Ida stayed in this pain until it began to fade. She continued to lie on the bed, feel- ing "drained"—but amazed at the experience she had just had. It was so different from any other time she had cried about Hank's un- availability, or when tears had occasionally come while talking with a friend about the fights her parents had had. Although she had cried at those times, the memory had seemed distant and sad. The ache in her stomach and the connection to Hank had not been involved. The previous experience had been like crying at a sad movie, whereas *this* time it was happening to her. She realized how many times, as an adult, she had felt that ache and had quickly acted to avoid it—so quickly, in fact, that she had not even noticed it. After a while, Ida got up. She felt a new lightness, and when she thought about Hank's distance, she felt no loneliness connected with it.

For several months the feeling kept returning and, each time, Ida went "into" it as she had the first time. She found that her childhood had been full of this loneliness, since her father was completely un-available to *anyone* on an emotional level and her mother was totally obsessed with struggling with her father. Ida had been an only child, but this fact was irrelevant to her feeling of loneliness: siblings cannot provide the connections children need with their parents.

Each time Ida processed this previously repressed childhood panic, she was grieving it. And each time, she felt less and less dis-tress about Hank's distance. After several months, Ida came to feel that she could manage perfectly well without Hank's attention—but she also realized that she had a choice about whether or not to stay in such a relationship. She felt no urgency to leave and was able to take her time to evaluate just what she was getting from this mar-riage and whether or not it provided enough of what she wanted for herself.

Doing the grieving makes the struggle unnecessary and gives us back our ability to process experience accurately. Ida was now in a position to see clearly what was true about Hank, both positive and negative, and to make a decision based on her best interest. Other issues might emerge as time went on, but each time she would be able to apply the processing techniques, find the childhood connections, grieve her losses, and free herself from that old, uncon-scious drive to struggle.

PROCESSING THE PAIN

This processing can be done in various ways, depending on the circumstances that exist when the old pain comes up. It can sometimes be a very subtle process, simply felt in private, with no outer evidence of what is happening. There will be times when you find yourself in the presence of others, where an emotional display would be inappropriate. In that case, all activity should remain a private, internal process, at least until you are out of that situation. Whenever possible, however, the regressive connecting process can be facilitated by some of the following techniques:

* Finding privacy or having someone who can sit quietly with you, doing nothing except being supportive.
* Lying down, on the floor if desired.
* Closing your eyes, feeling the pain, allowing any tears to flow freely.
* If you can "see" the memory that caused the pain, looking at the people who were there, causing it.
* If words from the feeling come to you—something the child you were needed to say but couldn't—looking at the person who is hurting you, and saying the words, out loud, in the present tense, directly to that person. For example, in Ida's regression, she might have called out through the bedroom wall at her father, "Stop it! Stop yelling at Mom—don't you know you are hurting me? Why don't you care about what's happening to me?" or to her mother, "Mommy, help me! Please come in to get me, I need you. Don't let Daddy hurt you like that. My stomach aches, help me, please Mommy, please . . ." over and over, as the hurt, needy, scared, five-year-old she was while in this regressed memory state.

There is often hidden pain connected to the words you would have said at the time of the trauma if they could have been articulated. This is so even if the painful experience is from infancy, before your cognitive ability was developed. Naming the feelings—putting words to them—can be enormously helpful in uncovering repressed pain.

When Ida began to feel and think more like the adult she was than the child she had been, she was in a position to consider her relationship with Hank rationally. As you may recall, Ida didn't feel compelled to push for answers or rush to a solution. The fact that she had no children made the situation less complicated for her, but it was the inner serenity that had been developed as she was more and more in her adult state that was principally responsible for her patient attitude. This did not develop overnight but took several months, some of which, at the beginning, were spent in an unconscious struggle.

Each such processing experience involves the effort to be consciously aware, as well as the willingness to stop defensive behaviors and feel emotional pain. However difficult and time-consuming this may be, the result is well worth it, as the healing that ensues is permanent.

chapter nine

Exercises in Aid
of Healing

The healing work we have discussed in the previous chapters requires time, energy, commitment, and a strong desire to overcome
the effects of an abusive childhood, in addition to an understanding
of the concepts involved. If you have read the preceding material
and wish to actively engage in the process, the following five exercises can provide you with helpful direction.

EXERCISE ONE: COMPILING AN ABUSE FACT LIST

Abuse

In order to increase your understanding of the various kinds of
abuse, I am repeating here, with some modifications, a selection of
the material presented by Pia Mellody* at the Second Annual Con-

---

*Pia Mellody is a consultant at The Meadows, a treatment center for addictions in Wickenburg,
Arizona.

ference of Adult Children of Dysfunctional Families, Santa Fe, New
Mexico, March 1988. Pia developed one of the first treatment programs in relation to the concept of "co-dependency." I've found
some of her work on the definition and organization of abusive experiences in childhood especially useful in helping people see
through their denial about the true meaning of what happened to
them.

Abuse is defined as "anything less than nurturing," or any action that "attacks the child's reality." The "child's reality" includes
her or his body, thinking process, feelings, and behavior.

Kinds of Abuse

Abuse can be discussed in different ways. First, we could talk about
whether the abuse is physical, sexual, or emotional, including what
is called "emotional incest." Physical abuse includes disrespectful
care of the child's body—beating, whipping, slapping, shaking,
banging the head, tickling until the child cries, pinching, too much
touching, and "witness abuse" (when a child has to watch another
child being abused or the parents abusing each other). Sexual abuse
can be incest, molestation, "flashing," voyeurism, suggestive or sexual talking, joking, leering, or name-calling, or refusal to grant physical privacy. Abuse that is emotional includes verbal mistreatment
(name-calling, screaming), demands for perfection, neglect, abandonment, and "overcontrolling reality" (telling the child what he or
she must wear, who his or her friends can be, how to think, what to
believe). "Emotional incest" is where a parent looks to one or more
of the children for relationship gratification that should be sought
from the spouse or another adult. According to Mellody, this is very
common in our society.

Another way to assess abuse is to look at whether the mistreatment is overt or covert, obvious or subtle. Physical abuse, with the
possible exception of too much touching, is overt, as is most verbal
emotional abuse. Some sexual abuse—incest, molestation, voyeurism, and flashing—is also overt. Sexually suggestive talking, joking,
name-calling, and leering and denial of physical privacy are covert,

as is the emotional abuse of neglect, abandonment, and demand for perfection.

Abuse can also be examined in terms of parenting styles. The abuse can be covert, such as treating the child with indifference, neglect, and behavior that is uncaring to the point of abandonment (even if it falls short of physically leaving the child). Covert abusive parenting can also refer to behaviors that exploit the child for the needs of the parents—inappropriate dependency (emotional incest) or pushing for some kind of success the parent never achieved—and what we call "enmeshment," a state in which the children are not allowed to be independent, responsible for themselves, but instead all family members are made to feel greater responsibility for the others than for themselves.

Abusive parenting can also be overt, in which case the child experiences open attacks, criticisms, and many forms of harsh treatment (ranging from being forced to eat for breakfast any part of a dinner left behind last night to actual physical torture).

Denial

In preparing to make a list of the abuse that you experienced in your childhood family, a careful review of the foregoing material can help. If, however, you are still in denial about what happened to you or how important it was, the denial can interfere with your ability to recognize the abuse even when you have the information describing abusive behaviors. There are certain ways of thinking or talking about the facts of childhood that indicate that denial is at work.

Before you attempt to determine family-of-origin abuse experiences, it is important that you assess your own thinking for signs of denial. I think of denial as the inability to realize—to make real—the truth. This can happen at any age, but denial of family truth starts in childhood and is necessary for our survival. The more we overcome this childhood denial, the more we will be able to realize the truth of our adult lives as well. Another definition of denial is: telling yourself a lie and *believing* it. Remember, denial is an unconscious process. When we know we are pretending something isn't true, it's not denial. It's very important to discover our own denial, so we can have a more conscious awareness of what is true.

To assist with this process, I have developed categories of denial and listed the kinds of things people say about their families under each category. These are not meant to be exhaustive, and there is some overlap, but they may help you recognize ways you have "explained away" facts about your childhood.

How to Recognize Denial

Most people, when discussing their childhoods, talk about them in a way that indicates that some form of denial is operating. It can be useful to know what kinds of statements you may routinely have been making about your experiences as a child in your family that show you are in denial. I have grouped these statements under headings that suggest what form of denial you are using when you say these things.

MINIMIZING: Minimizing occurs when you know what happened but you see it as having less of an impact than it did. When you minimize, you are likely to say:

"Other people had it a lot worse than I did."
"I know he or she or they . . . but it only happened sometimes."
"I never paid any attention to it."
"It didn't really bother me."
"I was never home, so it didn't affect me."

RESISTING: Resisting occurs when you know what happened but you believe it is irrelevant to your adult life. When you are resisting, you are apt to say something like:

"It was a long time ago."
"That was then, this is now."

"I came to terms with it (or made peace with
them) a long time ago."
"I've known it for years; I need to get on
with my life now."
"I don't have anything to do with them."
"That's just how it was."

OMITTING/BLOCKING: With omitting or blocking, you know only about
the pleasant parts of childhood, or you remember little or nothing.
When you are omitting or blocking, you are likely to say:

"I can't remember anything."
"I don't remember anything being wrong."
"I had a wonderful childhood, we went on
trips, etc."

BALANCING: In balancing, you know what happened but you think
that the "good things" balanced it out. As you do this, you might
say:

"I know he or she or they . . . but . . . I turned out OK."
"It made me strong (did me good)."
"We got everything we needed."
"I could always go to Mom (or Dad)."
"I (or We) knew they loved me (or us)."
"It built character."
"But they're good people."

EXCUSING/JUSTIFYING: In this form of denial, you admit the past but
find rationales for what happened. The things you will find yourself
saying when you are denying in this form might be:

"I (or We) deserved it."
"Everyone did it in those days."
"It was all he or she or they knew."

"We knew they loved us, they just couldn't show it."
"They did the best they could."

Recognizing some of the things you say or think about your family of origin may help you to identify more accurately the abusive things that happened there.

Bringing the Truth to Life

As you identify abuse in your family of origin, it can help to make a simple drawing using crayons or colored pencils. The colors you need are white (the background of a white sheet of paper will do), gray, red, yellow, and blue.

Draw a floor plan of the house you lived in as a child, including all the floors. If you lived in more than one house, draw the first one that comes to mind. Then color each of the rooms according to the feelings you remember having in them:

Red represents anger.
Gray represents loneliness.
White represents fear.
Yellow represents happiness/safety.
Blue represents sadness.

Feel free to use more than one color in a room. You may have the sense that you felt more than one way, at different times, in the same part of the house, so use as many of the colors as you need to represent each of the feelings.

This exercise may tell you things about your childhood experiences that you did not realize before. In a recent workshop I gave, one man used no colors at all; staring at his floor plan in amazement, he told the group, "I never realized how scared I was all the time as a child!" One of the women had colored her bedroom both white and yellow, depending on which parent tucked her in bed at night; another used red, gray, blue, and white through the various rooms in the house but colored her yard outside yellow, since she felt happy only when she was not inside the house.

Reviewing Your History

Once you have completed your drawing and considered your customary means of denial, you are ready to review your history in a more detailed way. Start by writing down, in paragraph form, the things you remember experiencing as a child. Record your age, who was there, and what happened. It is not necessary for this to be in chronological order. Next, write something about your parents' personalities—not as they might be now, in your adulthood, but as they were in relation to you and your brothers and sisters and to each other. Comment on how they spent their time; how much they were with the children; how you were treated by each of them; who made and who enforced the rules; who got to be angry and how; what happened during mealtimes, bedtimes, and after school; whether they abused or were addicted to substances; whether they were obsessed with work, sports, food, or cleanliness; what could be talked about and what could not; whether they showed affection toward each other and/or the children; whether some children were favored; whether ridicule, name-calling, or other "put-downs" were used; whether they were open about sharing their feelings and their histories with the children; whether there were extramarital affairs or other "secrets"; and so forth. As you do this, other specific experiences may come to mind. If so, add them to the previous description of your memories.

When you are finished describing your family, look over the history and description you have compiled and try to identify the abusive things that happened and the way your parents or other adults behaved that resulted in abusive experiences for you. When you are finished, go over your material with a friend who understands what denial is so that someone objective can detect where you might have presented something that was abusive as if it were OK.

Next, pick out the facts about your family that resulted in abusive experiences for you, and make a list. It should be composed of short paragraphs, stating what happened. Then shorten the descriptions to one or more phrases that embody the basic fact(s). Follow these phrases with the kind of abuse involved. When you are finished you will have your Abuse Fact List.

The following short paragraphs are examples of possible excerpts from different people's childhoods, with the information then shortened to the basic fact. The type of abuse is identified as it relates to the fact:

- Dad worked until late, and never wanted to be "bothered" when he got home. *Physically and emotionally unavailable father.* Type of abuse: COVERT/EMOTIONAL.
- Mom was always "sick" (hangovers, actually), and we kids could never make any noise that would bother her or Dad would hit us. *Absent alcoholic mother.* Type of abuse: COVERT/EMOTIONAL (Abandonment). *Father who hit us.* Type of abuse: OVERT/PHYSICAL. *Unreasonable limits set.* Type of abuse: COVERT/OVERCONTROLLING REALITY.
- Both Mom and Dad worked and I was always alone after school. I was supposed to have dinner ready for us when they got home. I couldn't ever play with my friends. *Left to care for self.* Type of abuse: COVERT/EMOTIONAL (Neglect). *Couldn't play with friends.* Type of abuse: COVERT/EMOTIONAL (Neglect).
- My much older sisters had to take care of me because my mom and dad both worked. They hated having to take me along with them while they were with their teenage friends and so were often crabby and mean. *Left in older sisters' care.* Type of abuse: COVERT/EMOTIONAL (Criticism, Faultfinding).
- I was the third oldest of seven kids. There was never enough time for any of us to get proper attention. *Too many kids, not enough attention.* Type of abuse: COVERT/EMOTIONAL (Neglect).
- My mom washed my mouth out with soap if I complained about something. She called it "talking back." *Mom washed mouth out with soap.* Type of abuse: OVERT/PHYSICAL (Inflicting physical pain).
- We were given enemas with too much water in them as punish-

ment for anything my dad didn't like. I was an adult in medical school before I knew an enema didn't have to hurt. *Dad tortured us with misused enemas.* Type of abuse: OVERT/PHYSICAL (Inflicting physical pain).

- We were beaten with switches that we had to go cut ourselves. *Beaten with switches.* Type of abuse: OVERT/PHYSICAL (Inflicting Physical Pain). *Had to cut them ourselves.* Type of abuse: OVERT/ EMOTIONAL (Anxiety-producing activity).

- Everyone in the family seemed nice, but whenever I tried to talk about anything that troubled me, Mom would change the subject. Dad was behind his paper. *Mom wouldn't let me feel bad.* Type of abuse: COVERT/EMOTIONAL (Abandonment). *Dad unavailable.* Type of abuse: COVERT/EMOTIONAL (Abandonment).

- My dad would come into my room at night and put his fingers into my vagina while he masturbated, from the time I was two until I was eleven, when my parents divorced. My mom must have known, and she didn't stop it. They divorced because he left her for another woman with two little girls, ages two and four. *Dad used me sexually.* Type of abuse: OVERT/SEXUAL (Incest). *Mom didn't stop him.* Type of abuse: COVERT/EMOTIONAL (Abandonment).

- My mom always wanted me to come straight home from school, discouraging me from sports and weekend stuff with my friends because she liked to talk to me about herself. She cried a lot and wanted to know I loved her. When I got into high school, I finally wouldn't listen to her anymore and did what I wanted, but I felt bad about it. *Mom used me for her emotional needs.* Type of abuse: COVERT/EMOTIONAL INCEST (Inappropriate dependence).

- Both Mom and Dad seemed to want to look at my body as I was developing my breasts. They wouldn't let me lock my bedroom or the bathroom doors, and just walked in on me, sometimes snickering. *Not allowed bodily privacy when "developing."* Type of abuse: COVERT/SEXUAL (Voyeurism). *Sexual development laughed at by both parents.* Type of abuse: OVERT/SEXUAL (Sexual ridicule).

- I could never wear the same clothes the other kids did. I would

hide things to change into on the way to school, buying them
with money I saved from my overly generous allowance. *Clothing dictated by mother.* Type of abuse: COVERT/EMOTIONAL
(Overcontrolling reality).

EXERCISE TWO: ADDING FEELINGS TO THE ABUSE FACT LIST

Since we are both mental and emotional beings, we respond both
mentally and emotionally to each of our experiences. Therefore, any
memories will have both a mental aspect (the picture we see when
we think about it, or the "fact") and an emotional aspect (how we
feel). When events have been repressed, it takes effort to remember
all or part of the experience; and when memories begin to return, we
often get in touch with one part first or more easily than the other.
In other words, some people remember what happened (the fact)
more readily, and others "remember" what it felt like (the feelings)
first. (Quotations are used here because people often do not recognize that memories can come in the form of feelings that are obviously out of context with the present. We have discussed this
phenomenon in relation to overreacting and symbolizing, but it is
also indicative of a repressed memory.) For clarity, we are separating memories into their two parts: the "fact" and the "feeling." To
the fact list you have already made, you will now be adding the corresponding feelings.

Recognizing Feelings

Because of repression, you may not be able to recall any feelings associated with the experience on your list. In fact, it is common not
to remember feeling anything in response to abusive situations. It is
helpful, therefore, first to determine which feelings a small child
could be expected to have in response to whatever experiences you
have listed as the facts. A general discussion about what feelings are
(and what they aren't) is in order here, as well as a reminder that
children are more deeply impacted emotionally by unloving experiences than we realize. In addition, it is important to recognize that,

with rare exceptions, certain feelings are experienced *only* in childhood. However, since most adults are in their childhood states of consciousness so much of the time (and unaware of it), we have come to think that feelings that actually belong in childhood are normal for adults to feel. At this juncture we need to come to a clear understanding of the difference.

In our culture, we often confuse feelings with thoughts, ideas, and attitudes. You may ask your friend, "What did that movie make you feel?" and hear in response, "It made me feel that we should pay more attention to the plight of the poor." But this answer is a thought, not a feeling. Basic feelings are simple and cause a physical reaction in our bodies. Many people are not connected to (aware of the physical sensations of) these primary human emotions and combine ideas with feelings. For example, someone who says he "felt like a failure" is combining a mental idea—that whatever happened made him less valuable as a person—with the physical pain of loss, usually resulting in sadness. Due to childhood experiences that resulted in certain ideas about what makes us worthwhile, good, approved of, safe, and so forth, we will not only feel whatever pure emotional pain should accompany a distressful experience, but we will attach some meaning to it as well. We are not aware that there are two separate processes involved here and thus come to think of the whole thing as "feeling."

Understanding what feelings really are, then, means separating the simple, basic emotion from any mental processes or ideas based on previous learning. It also means coming to know which feelings belong in our adult experience and which are felt now only because of our repressed childhood pain.

The most common basic feelings that adults would experience in the usual course of events, uninfluenced by ungrieved childhood pain, are:

Unpleasant	*Pleasant*
Anger	Joy
Rage	Contentment
Sadness	Safety

Unpleasant	*Pleasant*
Loneliness	Well-being
Fear	Love
Hatred	Happiness
Unhappiness	
Guilt	

Feelings normal to childhood, on the other hand, include all of the above, with the addition of the following unpleasant feelings:

Abandonment
Rejection
Inadequacy
Neediness
"Bad" or Wrong
Shame

Whenever adults feel abandoned, rejected, inadequate, or needy, they are feeling old, childhood feelings. It is only when people are dependent on others for their well-being that abandonment can take place. Adults can be "left," but when the resultant feelings are those a child would feel if left by the parent—such as panic, devastation, or disabling grief—it is not the present relationship loss that is being felt. Similarly, "rejection" is more than not being liked; it implies that we are faulty and reflects on our value, as does "inadequacy." As adults, we are adequate for some things and not adequate for others, and our sense of self-worth is not affected by this recognition. Feeling needy is a normal part of childhood, but when that feeling surfaces as an adult, it is old (as discussed in the charts showing the difference between childhood and adult reality in Chapter Three). All of these are old, childhood feelings that had to have occurred and been repressed; the unfelt pain is surfacing now, connected to the current event.

Some feelings—abandonment, rejection, inadequacy, neediness, "bad," and shame—are felt now, in our adult lives, *only* because we could not feel them as children. These are feelings that adults would not have if healthy maturation had occurred. No matter what the present circumstances, these are *always* old feelings when they are experienced in adulthood.

Guilt Versus Shame

The difference between "guilt," an adult feeling, and "shame," a childhood feeling, may need clarification. While guilt is an appropriate adult feeling, shame is not. Guilt is something we feel for one of two reasons. The first is our childhood conditioning, which taught us to believe that it is wrong for us to behave in a certain way. This could be something as innocuous as hurting Aunt Edna's feelings by saying no to a piece of pie we really do not want (or being honest in any other way with our families when we know they will not like what we have to say). If we have not yet decided for ourselves what our values are as opposed to what our parents taught us, we may still feel guilty when "breaking the rules." A second reason we feel guilty is because we have done something that violates our own values. In other words, we have broken our own rules.

In the former situation, we have an opportunity to resist the influence of our guilty feeling and act according to what we think instead of what we have been taught. If we do, we will gradually stop feeling guilty for things we don't believe are wrong. In the latter case, we need to evaluate what we have done, decide whether we were wrong and in what way, and take action to make amends for it if possible. We can accept responsibility and apologize if appropriate. Thus guilt is a helpful feeling in that it tells us when we have stepped off the track we want to be on, and it gives us an opportunity to correct our error.

In contrast to guilt, shame is a feeling that is caused by being treated as if we are bad when we are children. I believe that the concept of shame results from parents having been conditioned to believe that human beings have an innate tendency to be bad (which is not to say that bad adults do not exist). If the ability to feel a normal sense of wrongdoing has been damaged, destructive behavior will continue over time. It is common for badly abused or overly in-

dulged children to grow into adults with damaged ability to empa-
thize with or have compassion for anyone except themselves. Since
these people cannot feel guilt, motivation to correct themselves is
absent, and they will be likely to continue to act badly. People do
not, however, have inherently bad natures.

When parents respond to their children's human inadequacies
as if they are not simply mistakes or imperfections but acts due to
their inherent "badness" (an idea supported by the religion of the
majority in our society), they treat their children in ways that
cause a feeling of "shame" (badness). Because of the prevalence
of these beliefs and our own parents' response to us as children
based on these beliefs, we accept with the trust and innocence of
childhood that we have a shameful nature that has to be controlled
and that, when we fail to do so, we should feel what is called
"ashamed." My own experience with this feeling is one of utter
badness, beyond redemption—being someone no one could love.
It is my belief that the feeling of shame is created by childhood
mistreatment, while guilt is a normal feeling, to be experienced in
all phases of life.

Childhood Feelings Versus Adult Feelings

Before completing the exercise, it is important to spend some time
learning to differentiate what children as opposed to adults feel.
Paying attention to the feelings listed as normal to childhood can
help. It can also help to watch small children interact with their parents in places like the supermarket, beach, park, or other places families gather. When you see a child feeling something painful, try to
notice what caused it and what the child seems to be feeling in
terms of our list of the most simple human emotions.

Another thing to be considered is that, when describing
childhood feelings, we often use very big, adult words. "Abandonment" is an example. The child's wording would be "left."
"Rejection" would mean "not being liked." Many of the words we
use to describe feelings have simpler, child-related counterparts.
Try to determine those old, very young ways of saying how you

felt as a child when working with your childhood feelings. For instance, I remember saying I had an "owie" when I skinned my knee.

When you think you have increased your understanding of what a childhood feeling really is, take out your list of the abuses you experienced as a child in your family. Next to each abuse on the list, add the feeling you think you should have felt, whether you remember feeling anything or not. If you do remember feeling something, you should add that, too. It may be the same, or it may not be. Use the most childlike description of the feeling that seems appropriate.

The feeling additions to the previous Abuse List might look like this:

- Physically and emotionally unavailable father. Type of abuse: COVERT/EMOTIONAL. Feeling: *not good enough.*
- Absent alcoholic mother. Type of abuse: COVERT/EMOTIONAL (Abandonment). Feeling: *alone, not wanted.*
- Father who hit us. Type of abuse: OVERT/PHYSICAL. Feeling: *bad, scared, angry.*
- Unreasonable limits set. Type of abuse: COVERT/OVERCONTROLLING REALITY. Feeling: *bad, trapped.*
- Left to care for self. Type of abuse: COVERT/EMOTIONAL (Neglect). Feeling: *left, scared.*
- Required to cook family dinner. Type of abuse: COVERT/EMOTIONAL (Neglect). Feeling: *angry.*
- Couldn't play with friends. Type of abuse: COVERT/EMOTIONAL (Neglect). Feeling: *lonely, different.*
- Left in older sister's care. Type of abuse: COVERT/EMOTIONAL (Abandonment). Feeling: *not wanted.*
- Sisters were crabby and mean. Type of abuse: OVERT/EMOTIONAL (Criticism, Faultfinding). Feeling: *not liked, afraid.*
- Too many kids, not enough attention. Type of abuse: COVERT/EMOTIONAL (Neglect). Feeling: *forgotten, unimportant, not good enough.*

- Mom washed mouth out with soap. Type of abuse: OVERT/ PHYSICAL (Inflicting physical pain). Feeling: *scared, angry, bad.*
- Dad tortured us with misused enemas. Type of abuse: OVERT/ PHYSICAL (Inflicting physical pain). Feeling: *terror, rage.*
- Beaten with switches. Type of abuse: OVERT/PHYSICAL (Inflicted physical pain). Feeling: *fear, worthless.*
- Had to cut switches used to beat us. Type of abuse: OVERT/ EMOTIONAL (Anxiety-producing activity). Feeling: *fear, dread.*
- Mom wouldn't let me feel bad. Type of abuse: COVERT/EMOTIONAL (Abandonment). Feeling: *bad, wrong.*
- Dad unavailable. Type of abuse: COVERT/EMOTIONAL (Abandonment). Feeling: *ignored, not good enough.*
- Dad used me sexually. Type of abuse: OVERT/SEXUAL (Incest). Feeling: *bad, scared, ashamed.*
- Mom didn't stop him. Type of abuse: COVERT/EMOTIONAL (Abandonment). Feeling: *scared, bad.*
- Mom used me for her emotional needs. Type of abuse: COVERT/ EMOTIONAL INCEST (Inappropriate dependence). Feeling: *smothered, trapped, ashamed.*
- Not allowed bodily privacy when "developing." Type of abuse: COVERT/SEXUAL (Voyeurism). Feeling: *ashamed, embarrassed, angry.*
- Sexual development ridiculed by both parents. Type of abuse: OVERT/SEXUAL (Sexual ridicule). Feeling: *ashamed, embarrassed, angry.*
- Clothing dictated by mother. Type of abuse: COVERT/EMOTIONAL (Overcontrolling reality). Feeling: *sadness, anger.*

When your list is complete, review this work on the feeling part of your abuse experiences with another person—the same one you talked to about the first exercise, or someone else who understands the concepts we are dealing with here. It is important to have a supportive discussion, both to check against any tendency to be in denial and because we become more connected with our feelings when we talk about them with another person who is caring and respectful toward us.

EXERCISE THREE: MAKING A LIST OF SYMBOLIC REPRESENTATION

The completion of the second exercise has given you a concrete place to start in proceeding with this next step. Your goal here is to notice when you find yourself experiencing the feelings that are on your list from childhood. The ease with which you can do this will grow as your ability to observe your inner feelings objectively grows. It is necessary to be very aware of the bodily responses that childhood feelings evoke in order to maintain the separation between thoughts, attitudes, and emotions that we noted in the second exercise. Such subtle distinctions, although enormously significant, develop slowly for each of us. So be patient with yourself.

When beginning to look for these old feelings as they are to be found in your present, adult life, first review the list and spend some quiet time with each item, closing your eyes and letting yourself remember exactly how the feeling felt, and trying to find the words the child you were would have used for it. Try to experience it again as you are recalling it mentally. Get a firm sense of the feeling in your body, name it, and make a mental resolution to be aware enough to recognize that, when you experience this emotion again, it is the childhood feeling from your list.

Sometimes feeling in your body is not easily identified as anything other than tension perhaps in your shoulders or neck or abdominal area. As you concentrate on the tension, you may find it developing more clearly into an ache in your stomach, a feeling of pressure on your chest, or a sense that you have trouble breathing. You may realize that the tension, no matter where it localizes, is really something else, such as fear or anger. The ache in your stomach can also bring you to an awareness of some other feeling, such as sadness, loss, or loneliness. As you become more sensitive to the physical way your body shows emotional feelings, you may feel the physical pain of an emotional "heartache." The more you allow yourself to experience all the sensations that your body is holding, the more open you will become to the feeling reality of your childhood.

Connecting with Old Feelings

Some people have found a visualized "visit" into the home of their childhood helpful in getting connected to those old feelings.

Here is one such technique:

1. Get comfortable, close your eyes, relax, and take some deep breaths.
2. See yourself as the child you were (whatever age comes to mind), standing in front of the house you lived in with your family (whichever house occurs to you).
3. Visualize yourself enclosed in a clear bubble, one you can travel in and see out of, but in which you are protected from anyone else's feelings or actions.
4. Slowly move up to the door of your house, open it, and enter.
5. Proceed through the rooms of the house, slowly. Observe the rooms, their color, their furnishings, who is in them and what is going on. See yourself there and watch what is happening to you.
6. As you pass through the house, you may be different ages in different rooms. Let that happen. Stay in each room as long as you wish. Note what the child you were is feeling, or should be feeling.
7. When you are finished moving through the house, return to the front door, open it, and exit.
8. Return to the place in front of the house where you started and get out of the bubble.
9. Feel yourself in your body as the adult you are, and, when ready, open your eyes.

A variation is to do the same imagery but without the protective bubble. If you try this, try to be "in the body" of the child you were, feeling the feelings as much as possible. The principles that apply here are the ones discussed when explaining the regressive process in Chapter Eight. As you may recall, emphasis was placed on surrendering to the experience and whatever feelings are brought up by it. Fear is to be expected, since that was always part of any event that was severe enough to result in repression; but this, too, belongs in the past and should not inhibit the willingness to "give in" and allow yourself to experience whatever happens as totally and defenselessly as possible.

After preparing yourself, spend a significant portion of time looking for these feelings in your life. Keep daily notes about when you felt the feeling and what person or situation brought it up. (Notice I did not say "caused it," since people and events in our adult lives do not actually cause these feelings—they just tap into our unconscious in a way that results in the previously blocked emotion, usually painful, emerging into our present experience.)

It is important to take the time over a period of weeks to observe your emotional responses and keep a record of when, with whom, and what you feel about those old, painful feelings. This will most likely be difficult. In order to accomplish this successfully, you must set aside any ideas and opinions you have regarding key issues in your present life, and temporarily suspend any actions you have been taking, or thinking of taking, based on your evaluation of these issues. Conclusions about things currently happening in your life (jobs, relationships, etc.) are often a hodgepodge of unrecognized old feelings, unconscious attempts to get childhood needs met, and inaccurate processing of experience (as discussed in Chapter Six). Suspending this activity for the time being will not interfere with the achievement of whatever you perceive your goals to be; but, if you are like most people, you will be afraid that it will. Again, it is important to trust the potential gain from doing this work enough to be willing to experiment.

It isn't necessary for you to be aware *at the time of the interaction* that an old feeling has been brought up. It doesn't matter if you don't realize it until some time later. Write it down, no matter when this event happened, or how much later you become aware of it. At this point, your goal is to discover where every feeling on your Fact Feeling List is experienced in your life now, and what or who brings it up.

To illustrate, let's consider Tom, who often noted the feelings of being "not good enough," "unimportant," or "not wanted" on his Feelings List. Tom's log might look like this:

March 4: Tried to ask boss question during time he was involved with something else. Was reacted to irritably and asked to come back later. Felt unimportant.

March 8: Wanted attention from Kim when she came home late last night. She basically ignored me, just going to sleep. Felt unwanted.

March 9: Kim again. She got angry when I tried to talk to her while she was fixing dinner. Unimportant.

March 16: Numerous times this week, noticed that Kim often preferred to read or call a friend on the phone rather than talk with me. Felt not good enough.

March 18: Jim didn't want to take the time to arrange for our next tennis game. Felt not good enough.

March 25: Found out that Jim did not invite me to hunting trip he planned. He knows I don't like to hunt, but I felt not good enough anyway.

Tom can begin to note from these incidents that Jim, Kim, and his boss may be primary symbols for him.

For Susan, whose childhood feelings were often those of being needy and afraid, the log might look like this:

June 8: Edith was playing the stereo really loud and I was afraid our picky neighbors would be angry. She just laughed at my concern, even though I began to fear the police might be called. Felt like I needed someone to stick up for me so I wouldn't be hurt, but no one would. Felt afraid and needy.

June 12: I realized today how loud and boisterous Edith tends to be and that whenever we are in public together, I feel fear, as if something bad is going to happen. I also wish that someone was there who was capable of handling the situation I'm afraid might arise. Feelings of being both needy and afraid are always present; I just never noticed them.

June 15: Today I wondered if the reason I love my job at the library might be because it is always so quiet, so I am never afraid.

Susan can see that anyone "too" boisterous or a noisy situation (which may have influenced the job choice) made her uncomfortable because of the childhood feelings that were aroused.

When you have done your logging and have gathered enough information to see the emergence of obvious patterns, you are ready to make your Symbolic Representation List. It may be helpful to list people separately from situations. You may also want to list them in order, with the ones to whom you respond most often or most strongly at the top.

For example, Tom's list might look like this:

SYBMOL	FEELING
Kim	Unimportant
	Unwanted
	Not good enough
Boss	Unimportant
Jim	Not good enough

Susan's might look like this:

SYMBOL	FEELING
Edith	Afraid (of making someone angry)
	Needy for protection
Library job	Keeps me "safe" (avoid fear)

EXERCISE FOUR: MAKING A SYMBOLIC DEFENSE LIST

The next step is to spend more time observing yourself and your responses, but this time with the focus on your behavior. Now that
you have a list of the people and situations that are symbolic for you
and the childhood feelings they evoke in you, it is time to clarify
your usual automatic behavioral response. This, too, should be noted
on a daily basis: what happened and with whom, the feeling it
brought up, what you did in reaction.

By now, you should be accustomed to observing and noting
the first two events. The purpose of adding your reactions is to
clarify your typical defensive responses to your symbols. (These
are the "struggle" or "shut-down" reactions we discussed in Chapters Three and Four.) When you have identified your typical defensive response behavior, it should be added to the list, in its
simplest form, next to the name of the person and/or the event that
brought it up: "I yell," "I cry," "I argue," "I walk away," "I clam
up," "I act as if nothing happened," "I say I'm sorry," and so
forth.

After you have observed yourself sufficiently to have a good
awareness of what behavioral reactions you usually have to each
symbol and the old feeling it brings up, you will have completed
your Symbolic Defense List, with its three components. It might
look like this:

SYMBOL (person or event and what is happening)	FEELING (old)	DEFENSE (reaction)
Mary complains	Anger	Read the paper
Boss is irritable	Fear	Smile, tell a joke
Mother criticizes	Bad	Argue with her
Daughter's feelings are hurt	Sad	Tell her it's nothing to cry about

Or course, your list may be much longer.

EXERCISE FIVE: ACTIVATING THE GRIEF PROCESS

As we have seen, grieving is more complicated than thinking, talking, or crying about the past. In Exercise Five, we will use a three-part process to overcome our unconscious defenses and begin to grieve.

Part One

The first step involves learning to disconnect from a symbol at the time you usually engage in defensive behavior (withdrawal, avoidance, struggle). Your Symbolic Defense List gives you information and structure that will be helpful in accomplishing this task.

"To disconnect" means to recognize that what is happening is symbolic for you, and you either are about to respond or are already responding, defensively—either by struggling or by shutting down. After recognizing this, you reverse yourself; in other words, you change the direction of your attention. Up to now, you have been focusing on what has happened in your adult, present environment. Understanding that you are responding to a symbol can allow you to remove your attentive energy from the external, symbolic event and refocus it inward. It is the removal of the energy from the present event that is meant by "disconnecting."

Reversing yourself when you are in the grip of a very strong impulse involves mental and emotional discipline. You must plan ahead, which is where the Symbolic Defense List can be helpful. As you become very familiar with who or what is symbolic for you and how you usually defend yourself, you can then be prepared for the next encounter. You must keep your mind on what you expect could happen, and what you will do when it does. You make a commitment to yourself that you will behave in a certain way, decided in advance, rather than do what you usually do. Then you follow through on your commitment even if your thoughts or feelings tell you to do something different at the time. It may help to remember the moves required to control a skidding car: although it feels wrong to do so, you must turn the steering wheel in the direction of the skid rather than away from it. None of us are used to turning right to go left. It goes against everything our bodies want to do when we are skidding, but we force ourselves to remember the driving instructor's dictum, trusting the correcting thing will happen—and it does. Downhill skiing on a steep slope is another example. Our bodies want to lean back toward the uphill side of the mountain out of fear, but the correct thing to do—the thing that will keep us from falling—is to lean out, over our skis, facing downhill, as if we are going to fly.

You must have already evaluated whether the action you are deciding to substitute for your defensiveness can possibly hurt you in any way because reversing yourself involves the same trusting kind of control that skiing or reacting to a skid does. Following through and effecting this reversal makes the disconnection possible.

This does not necessarily mean that you are not still "seeing" the person who is your symbol, or still thinking about him or her, but it does mean that you have become aware that the energy actually belongs somewhere else, in your past. You become focused on the energy itself (facts and feelings) rather than continuing to think obsessively about a present outcome.

Part Two

After you have disconnected from the present struggle, the energy that has been directed outward must be used to examine your inner state. The feeling that you have been trying to avoid through defenses is what you need to search for. This is why removing your attachment to the present event is so important. Without doing so, you cannot be in the receptive state necessary to open to your painful emotion.

This second part may take some time. You probably will not be successful at first. If you are able at least to drop your defenses and attempt to find the feeling, even if you cannot feel it the first several times, you will be accomplishing a great deal. Inevitably, if you continue the attempt, you will become aware of the feeling. When this happens, it is important to firm up the sense of the feeling, as we have discussed in Exercise Three.

Part Three

After you have a firm sense of the painful feeling that you have thus far defended yourself against, try to reconnect it to the original event or truth that caused this pain. It will most likely be in your family, as a child, but this original source may not be directly available.

An event may just "float into" your mind. If this happens, great: close your eyes, take yourself back by visualizing yourself as the child you were, and stay with the pain and the old reality as long as you can.

If you cannot connect your feeling so readily, however, there are two ways you can try to help the process. First, you can ask yourself when you've felt this feeling before. Then ask yourself when else, and so forth, going back in time until you have come to the earliest recollection you have. Each time you try it you may find yourself remembering earlier and earlier times. Next, ask yourself what words fit the way you are feeling. For instance, you may be feeling very alone. Imagine what you might want to say based on that feeling; it might be "Why wasn't someone here for me?" or "I need someone with me." If words come to you, they are most likely a description of the exact circumstance that caused the feeling in the first place. Saying them out loud can sometimes enable you to "drop into" the old memory.

Sometimes you will not be able to find the memory and make the reconnection. For some people, in fact, just the attempt to do so can cut off the pain. If you find that you lose the feeling when you try to reconnect with your childhood reality, stop the attempt. Staying connected with the painful feelings is most important. If anything you attempt disconnects you from them, stop and go back to what you were doing when you were feeling them. For most people, that would be to focus on the present symbol. If you find that you cannot "stay in the feeling" without thinking about or "seeing" the symbol, then keep doing it. The important thing is that you know the pain belongs somewhere in your childhood, regardless of who you think is causing it now, and you remain open to any shift back to the past reality that might happen without your effort.

Let's review the steps again. To reiterate:

1. Disconnect your focus from the symbolic person or happening.
2. Find the painful feeling that symbol is bringing up and get a firm sense of it. Let it affect you.
3. If possible, reconnect the feeling with the original event or reality from childhood that caused it. If the feeling fades with such an attempt, stay focused on the symbol, remembering that it is just that, a symbol of someone or something else.

Once you have developed the ability to engage this three-part response to symbolic events instead of using your old defenses, you will have reached the childhood state of consciousness that allows you to grieve that old pain now and heal it.

Again, while feeling your pain fully, letting it hurt you, and revisiting the childhood situation that created it, you may experience a great deal of anguish. Allowing that to happen—weeping when your tears flow, crying out the words of the feeling, "seeing" your family members, being "back there" as you visualize it, being "in the body" of the child you were—makes it possible for the energy of the child's unfelt pain to flow through you, undefended, unchecked. It may seem as if it will never stop.

But it does. When allowed to be felt fully, with no timetable, no attempt to control or judge it as "too much," it stops all by itself. It stops, you rest, and then, as some of that old pain is healed, a bit of your adult reality becomes available to you, as something new, unknown before; at the same time, what really happened to you "back there" becomes clearer as well as what your real needs are now.

Many people find that a soothing, comfortable calm engulfs

them after this emotionally wrenching experience. Sometimes it feels good just to be "bathed" with this calm. Or, as in the example of Julie, who decided during such a respite that she wanted to put a picnic together and take the children out, something that feels good to do with your emerging "self" may occur to you. Be sure to follow these urges; they are the real you.

This is the process, to be repeated for as long as necessary. Each time will produce a greater awareness of the truth of what was done to you in your childhood, as well as what is really true about today. Each grief experience will allow you to spend more and more time in adulthood before you are thrown back into your pain by a symbol as yet not resolved.

Many therapies today attempt to help people feel the pain of their childhoods, or do "memory retrieval work." The experience I've described here is different in that it includes the present reality context that you have unconsciously created to continue your struggle or avoidance defensiveness. When this context is not used as a starting point, the emotional experience you have, even though experienced as a satisfying relief, is not complete, and your unconscious program of "hope" that you can change the past (through symbols) will continue. The identification and use of your present-day symbols is a crucial part of this therapy, helping to ensure that the result of your regressive visit to your childhood will include the truth behind the feelings, so you will know who it was who hurt you, and how, and that you were an innocent victim of this. Then, relieved of the need for symbolic relationships or defenses, you will be able to see what your real, adult needs are now. This is crucial, because only then can you make real efforts to meet your authentic adult needs. Sometimes you will be successful, sometimes not, but even when you fail, another choice is always there. In the unconscious attempt to change your childhood, failure is certain.

This process is very difficult. There will be times when you think you cannot stand to feel the pain. You will think it's just "too hard." It *is* hard, but it is possible, and it is endurable. You can stand it, it's the child you were who couldn't. The mechanism that allows us to do this work, difficult as it is after all these years, is a wonder. And more wonderful is the fact that the healing it leads to is permanent.

chapter ten

Trusting the
Regression Process

Regression work is hardest in the first few months. Whereas people often leave currently popular treatment centers or workshops feeling better, adherents of therapy that uses regression report that it is difficult, painful, exhausting. However, many of those who have undergone other therapies have found that when the "feel better" glow fades, neither their symptomology nor much else in their lives has changed.

In my office, I have a poster of a Raggedy Ann doll being put through the wringer of an old-fashioned washing machine. Her body is halfway through, so she is hanging, flattened and limp, from the waist down. The caption for the poster, "*The Truth Will Make You Free, But First It Will Make You Miserable*," gains significance for my clients as their work progresses.

Therapy based on the real answers—the simple ones, as found here—doesn't make people feel better right away. Initially, they feel worse! Thus many people run from it. More than once a new client who has been referred by a long-term client will see me two or three times and then quit. I then hear from my client that the friend has

said, "I know Jean is right, but I don't want to face it." This is understandable. No one wants to feel bad. But it is important that those
of you who are ready for such an undertaking understand which
type of therapy can get you where you want to go and which cannot,
so you can make an informed choice.

Only a therapy that is based on the simple truth of what really
happened in your childhood—uncovering it, dropping denial, overcoming repression, and facing the devastating pain it put you in
when you could not acknowledge it and still live—will ultimately be
effective. To face the facts fully, to feel the pain, and to recognize
the source of these wrongs and the legitimacy of your needs—
without being encouraged to "forgive," create an alternative reality,
or depend upon a group process—will enable you to heal.

REFUSING THE "ADULT VERSUS CHILD" GAMBIT

We have already discussed some of the difficulties inherent in doing
this work—the strength of the urge to struggle or withdraw, the fear
that will beset you, and, of course, the unavoidable suffering en-
tailed in allowing yourself to feel the old pain itself—but there is yet
another common response that can impede you, this time a mental
one.

The difference between your childhood state of consciousness
and your adult state can never be understood until it is no longer a
concept but an experience. Until it has happened to you, not once,
but many times, you will only be able to believe it to be so; you will
not know it for yourself. During the period of time when you have
not yet felt yourself to be that child consciously and have not yet
grieved enough of your old pain to actually realize your adult state,
you will be in danger of trying to decide what is "adult" and what
is "childhood." This is especially the case when your symbol is a
love partner, for it is in intimate relationships that it is hardest to
live with uncertainty. Let me explain.

It is not unusual for my clients to be struggling with someone
who is unavailable in some way. When directed into the childhood

pain that is symbolized by their relationship, the client will often de-
flect the attention from regression, asking, "But wouldn't an adult
want closeness?" It can be confusing to be told that you are reacting
from your childhood state of consciousness in other symbolic situations as well. Let's say you feel great shame upon overhearing a
derogatory remark about an article of clothing you are wearing at a
party. After making an immediate departure from the party, making
sure your exit was not observed, and crying all the way home—
behavior obviously prompted by childhood feelings—you might
ask, "But what would an adult have done?"

This question is common and indicates understandable and legitimate initial confusion. However, it is important to recognize
three things. First, spending any time trying to figure out what your
adult behavior would have been had you felt like the adult you are
instead of the child you were misdirects your focus and stalls the
healing work. Second, asking such a question indicates an attempt
to control the situation by taking an emotional "shortcut." In other
words, this question can come from an unconscious desire to avoid
feeling the pain by discovering how to think and behave like an
adult without going through the grieving necessary to get there.
Third, just as there is no generic "child" that we all were, there is
no collective "adult." Just as each childhood was different, each of
us has become a unique adult self. Thus *you cannot know how you
will feel and think and what you will do as the adult you truly are
until you are fully in that state of consciousness.*

An even greater danger exists if you try to make decisions
about your present life before reaching your adult state of consciousness. The idea that your feelings and attitudes about certain
aspects of your life can actually be entirely a result of unconscious
motivation due to unmet childhood needs is very difficult to accept
at all, but most particularly when you are being buffeted by old
pain. Most of us will go through a period when we believe our pain
about someone's unavailability is old and should be grieved, but at
the same time cling to the idea that at least *some* of what we are
feeling is caused by the present situation. This is dangerous because
we cannot grieve halfheartedly. Once a person in your life is iden-

tified as a symbol, then you must accept, at least as a hypothesis, that *all* the hurt you feel in response to that person is actually childhood pain.

Accepting something as a hypothesis means that you suspend judgment on whether it is true or not long enough to test it out. During the trial time, you need to act as if the hypothesis were true, and the results of your actions will prove whether it is true or not. With regression work, the test takes a minimum of several months. It is during this time, when you are first in the process of dropping defenses and feeling your pain, that you might be tempted to try to figure out what is present and what is old, because it takes so much time for the process to unfold. Once you feel the first shift into your true adult state of consciousness and see the difference in how you feel and think about the same thing that was just hurting you, the desire to sort out past from present diminishes.

We can see this in action in many cases. For instance, Jackie had fits of jealousy whenever her boyfriend, Paul, wanted to spend an evening "alone." She never believed that he genuinely wanted some time on his own until she remembered and experienced the way her older sister had lied to her to get rid of her so she could be with her friends. Before this shift into the childhood state, Jackie was sure that "anyone" would be jealous. Now she finds that she's the one who wants to spend more time alone. Similarly, although Dan had left a woman he was very attracted to because she was abusive to him, he nevertheless had a hard time not following her home whenever he saw her car. Since his feelings were so strong, he feared that maybe he had made the wrong decision after all—until he experienced the pain triggered by knowing that the closest he had got to being loved as a child was to be abused. After that recognition, even seeing the woman accidentally was not a problem for Dan.

TRUSTING IN THE RETURN OF THE ADULT STATE

Another factor that should be considered in regard to decision-making is that when you are in a childhood state you will have only the mental and emotional abilities of the child you were. Your ability to relate to a problem rationally will revert back to that of the earlier age to which you have regressed. You cannot be in both states at the same time. You can "stay adult" only to the extent that you can recognize that the fear and pain you are feeling is not due to present circumstances, and therefore must be "taken back" and experienced as totally as possible. Other than that awareness, your adult ability to evaluate and judge a situation will be unavailable to you. You must wait until it returns.

In certain repetitive symbolic situations, like Brian's desire for Kathy's undivided attention, Peter's need to protect himself from what felt like Julie's intrusiveness, or Ida's need for Hank's companionship, it will take a very long time for the adult state to be experienced at all. A guideline that can be used during this period is to accept as old anything you are thinking or feeling about those aspects of your relationships that have been identified as symbolic, and to recognize as a defense any tendency you may have to question that.

THE WILLINGNESS TO GRIEVE

Much of what you will need to do at first involves overcoming defenses, since grieving is not possible until that is accomplished. Grieving is a state of total defenselessness in which you need to surrender to whatever you know to be the truth, no matter how it impacts on you emotionally. As a child, you could never do this. As an adult, regressed to the child you were, you can. Feeling the old pain that was never processed allows you to know what was really true about your family of origin, to admit what happened and how bad it was, and to reclaim your memories. Grieving these memories neutralizes them. They become pictures from your past that once hurt you but happened long ago and are now over. Grieving enables you truly to be in your adult life, with full awareness. Your ability to process experiences as they happen without unconscious interference, with which you were born, will then return to you; you will be able to make decisions and choices based on what is really true about your adult reality, instead of reacting to what happened to you

as a child. This doesn't mean that you won't have pain: much of
what happens to us as human beings, capable of conscious awareness and emotions, is painful. But you won't need to try to avoid
what hurts you, or deny the truth in that attempt.

The willingness and ability to grieve will give you gifts far beyond the healing of your abusive childhood. As we move through
our lives, continuing to grieve when hurts happen, we are able to
face painful truths instead of denying them and experience that same
healing power in the present. R. D. Laing is quoted as saying, "Life
has a lot of pain that cannot be avoided. The only pain that can be
avoided is the pain that comes of trying to avoid pain." In authentic
adult reality, our problems are not caused by distressing events but
by our perceived need to avoid the emotional impact of what happens to us. Although doing so will hurt at times, once we are free
to face reality squarely, the ability to open to pain and grieve it allows us to make sensible and effective decisions about how to handle any situation in a way that is healthy for us.

Mary, for instance, can see how Joe is drinking more and being
abusive to her. She will know how she feels—probably both angry
at and disappointed in him. It will be clear what her options are at
this point, and she can choose among them. Confronting Joe with
his behavior and insisting that he take responsibility for stopping the
excessive drinking and the abusive behavior is one of them. Failing
that, she can leave Joe; fortunately, she is not dependent on Joe's income for support. Or, if she chooses, she can stay and make the best
of it, but she will know that it was her choice and will not fall prey
to underlying resentments. Free from the effects of having to repress
her childhood abuse, Mary will be unhappy about the situation, but
she will be able to respond to it according to present reality.

RECLAIMING OUR LIVES

Most of us have lived for years with some kind of unhappiness:
emotional narrowness; unending, unquenchable efforts to excel or
"succeed"; worrying what other people think of us; obsessing about
the last interaction we had, having "conversations" in our heads;

feeling dead inside; being afraid of people; isolating ourselves; lying to hide who we are; never finding work we like or coworkers with whom we can get along; committing ourselves to someone we're sure is the "love of our life," only to have the feelings go flat after a while; feeling disappointed in ourselves as parents, or in our children; carrying anger, blame, and resentment around with us . . . The list can go on and on.

Why are so many people obsessed with the power and control that wealth (or battering) can provide? Why is there so much fighting and hatred in our world? Why do members of one religious or ethnic group kill members of other groups? Why are so many people diagnosed as "clinically depressed"? Why are mood-altering drugs in such demand?

Obviously, we are not quite "sane." Something deep inside us has not been satisfied. I believe that "something" is the infant's need for love. The child you were can never get that love—nothing will satisfy that deep need. But grieving has the power to heal us—to make us whole again and to let us reclaim our lives.

This is the way for real sanity to return. We will not always be happy: life gives us a full range of experiences, some of them very painful. But once we have consciously returned to the most deeply painful events of our own childhoods and come to be aware of all that was hidden, we cannot hurt others without feeling their pain too. We will no longer believe that power or wealth can give us anything truly important. We will not be able to live with anything less than the truth, for ourselves and others. And the best part is, the more sanity we attain, the more peaceful we become.

appendix a

Regression Therapy and Other Childhood Healing Methods: Comment and Caution

Since the release of this book in April, 1995, I have received many telephone calls and letters from people in the United States, Canada, Australia, several European and Scandinavian countries, and Israel. Occasionally a reader has traveled to the Idaho valley where I live for a week of face-to-face therapy, followed up by telephone work. For most people this is, of course, impossible, so I have offered those unable to travel some guidelines to follow as they continue in their own particular situation.

I have also heard from several therapists inquiring about using this therapy with their clients, but only a few have recognized the necessity of experiencing their own childhood pain. The majority of therapists who become engaged by this book seem interested only in using it as one of many "methods" in an eclectic style of working.

Such a view indicates a misunderstanding, since there can be no compromise between therapies that proceed as if unconscious-mind states do not influence us, and this therapy, which clearly distinguishes between the unconscious (childhood reality) state of mind and the conscious (adult reality) state of mind. In addition, the practice of this therapy demands an expertise based on knowledge arising from the therapist's own explorations of his inner self, not methods based on someone else's theories. In order to lead clients into the regressive work outlined in this book, the therapist must know, through his own experience, what childhood realities are like behind the repressive barrier.

I advise people seeking help in doing this therapy on their own to use the exercise portion of this book with a friend who wants to try it as well. If that is not possible, I suggest that they find a therapist with whom they feel comfortable as a person, give her this book, and ask her to read it. If the therapist responds positively to the concepts presented, the client can then ask her whether she would be willing to be a companion through the process, forgoing her usual methods.

Coping with fear is a topic that frequently comes up in my conversations with readers: People tend to "believe" the fear experienced during regression therapy and interpret it as a message that the amount of pain they are feeling is dangerous. Although this subject is covered more than once in the body of the text, I cannot emphasize it enough: For a physically healthy adult who is not suffering from a mental illness causing psychosis, there can be no emotions "too painful" or dangerous to feel. When we, as adults, find ourselves terrified that our emotional pain will somehow damage or overwhelm us to the point of being unable to "function," it feels true (now) because it *was* true (then). It's important to understand, using the intellectual function of our adult mind, that we are in no danger, regardless of how much it feels as if we are. This is the difference between the past (child's) reality and the present (adult's) reality. Being aware of these two different time frames simultaneously allows us to have the courage to experience something that feels as if it will kill us. The rule of thumb in regressive therapy is that *nothing that hasn't already happened can happen now.* The pain can no longer "hurt" us unless we agree to take harmful action against ourselves. *This we must not do,* understanding that the desire to do so is a part of our childhood that has been repressed, and when we allow ourselves simply to feel it, it passes. The reader who needs additional support in managing her fear may find it helpful to review the sections listed in the index under "fear."

Readers also have questions concerning the similarity or difference between this therapy and other therapies dedicated to the healing of childhood-abuse pain. Although space does not permit a thorough comparison, I feel I should comment, however briefly, on some important fundamental differences.

Although the term "Regression Therapy" in the subtitle of this book has been used in the context of other therapies, it is used here to describe a very different experience. I want to inform the reader that any therapy involving aggressive "memory retrieval," or dramatic, emotional group experiences claiming to "heal" any particular aspect of one's painful childhood relationships or experiences, is not the same as the work outlined in this book.

One difference is important enough to highlight here: In these emotionally charged, therapist-guided experiences, childhood is focused on to the exclusion of present-day, symbolic relationships in which repressed, unprocessed aspects of participants' childhood experiences are currently—and unconsciously—being re-created. Parental relationships are explored without the necessary distinction being made between the nature of that relationship as it *was*, child to adult, and the relationship that exists *now* adult to adult. In other words, the mother or father of your childhood and the way you were treated by her or him exists in a different time frame and consciousness from the relationship you have with either of them now. People come out of these therapies and workshops claiming to have "healed" the relationship with a parent, both past and present, but symbolic relationships (with a romantic partner, boss, etc.), in which old, unmet needs are still actively influencing the perceptions and emotions, continue unchanged.

Another approach to healing also causes me concern: some therapists encourage clients to "accept their feelings" without needing to explain or understand them. They are emphasizing that feelings are valid in and of themselves, just because one has them. The purpose is an attempt to overcome societal prejudices against emotion and to release the stigma attached to feelings in childhood that parents considered "unjustified." Well intentioned as it may be, this reasoning is flawed, since it does not take into consideration the fact that feelings come from two different reality levels, or states of consciousness. As therapists we have to understand that in order to do genuine regressive work, it is necessary to step aside from what might otherwise be supportive and valid advice in order to identify a feeling that is actually coming from a time frame in the past and thus has nothing to do with the present. Feelings that have their source in childhood are *valid*, but not as an appropriate response to present-day situations.

Success in regression therapy is attained when the client can distinguish whether his thoughts and feelings are occurring in response to past (childhood) events or whether they are truly a reasonable reaction to present circumstances. With that knowledge in place, any painful feeling that is brought up from the unconscious in response to a symbol can be recognized for what it is—valid only in terms of the past, childhood-abuse reality. It must be felt for what it is, not indiscriminately encouraged by a therapist's "go ahead, have your feeling" approach.

Another form of therapy that deserves comment is "rage work." It is the focus of some short-term residential workshops, and the idea is that one can "reduce" one's rage by expressing it. As healing work must begin with a present-day discomfort to be effective, and must be done with conscious awareness of how the past is unconsciously represented in the present, "rage reduction" work can provide only temporary relief at best. (In the main text of this book, I explain that rage is actually a bottom-line defense against childhood powerlessness and that it is the powerlessness itself that needs to be experienced.)

As a result of Alcoholics Anonymous and other Twelve-Step programs that influence the contents of most popular "recovery" publications, "spirituality" (a fundamental Twelve-Step concept) is now considered a necessary part of the healing process. Emotional reliance on a "higher power" is encouraged, particularly when facing painful memories. I believe this is a serious mistake: When painful childhood feelings emerge, we are experiencing a time in our lives when we were too young to understand spiritual concepts, and, in most cases, we were alone with our *pain*, with no one to lean on. This is part of the reality that *needs to be experienced,* unmitigated by an adult concept.

Another negative phenomenon, perhaps also due to the influence of Twelve-Step programs, is that many people who are attempting to heal from childhood wounds are being told to beware of feeling like a victim. One approach is to see the "victim feeling" as a character flaw that must be overcome (with higher-power help); another goes so far as to teach that each of us "chose" our abusive parents so we could receive the experience we needed in this lifetime to "grow" (another aspect of the spirituality approach).

These approaches are misguided in two ways: First, the concepts of symbolism and the automatic shift into childhood states of consciousness are not understood, and therefore not available to be worked with. Second, the implicit directive not to blame our parents interferes with our ability to access appropriate feelings and corresponding realities from our histories. The fact is that abused children *are* victims, and *when we are in a childhood state,* we *must* be able to be, in our feelings, the victims we were. Under the influence of the no-blame approach, this vital information is missed, and as a result, people attempting to heal from childhood abuse may well add current self-judgment and shame to their list of problems, since working with childhood pain will inevitably at some point cause them to feel like the victims they all were.

Those who become aware of the damage caused by their parents sometimes start wanting or expecting them to "fix" it. Therapists must help their clients understand that it is the child they were who is the victim, and it is the adult they are who needs to take responsibility for healing. No one else can. The wish for justice or redress must be exchanged for the reality of loss and the pain of grief. People can be encouraged to relinquish a present victim identity by being helped to understand that they do have a right to those feelings—as they apply to the past. In order for this to happen, the shift back to the childhood state of mind must be recognized, by both therapist and client.

Another error found in other healing methods is the belief that the client needs to somehow "make himself safe" in order to face past realities. A process called "guided visualization"—a gentle hypnotic technique—is used to enable the client to "create" a safe place in his mind. The place is often somewhere in nature, surrounded with the beauty and serenity of trees, fields, streams, or lakes. The client is told that he can return to this place whenever he is frightened, so he will "know" he is safe—that there is a refuge—when "things" (regressive experiences, presumably) become "too much." What this does, in fact, is confirm the unconscious belief on the part of the client that he is not safe even now, when the dangers of childhood are long over. This is antithetical to reality: The client *is* safe—fears are old feelings and need to be felt as such (as discussed in Chapter 8).

Finally, another concept I am concerned about is the popular belief that it is requisite to the healing process to understand and forgive the abuser. I think that this is related to the need to protect parents from being "blamed." Regressive techniques are being used to create fantasy dialogues with family members of childhood, the goal being to understand that they, too, were abused children. As true as that may be, regressive methods must be used to help us feel *the truth of what happened,* not to impose a moral or religious code to create in imagination something that never happened. Maybe someday, after much healing has occurred, the adult we are will feel forgiving toward the people who abused us as children—maybe not. The child we were, however, was in no position to deal with the concept, since the relationship we had with our caregivers was never one of equal power.

As the adults we are (and I hope this book had helped you to realize the difference), we *now* have as much power as our parents. It is this very power that *gives us the right* to forgive them or *not,* as we please, once we have accessed the truth. For anyone with the authority a therapist wields to impose the moral value of "forgiveness" as a precept for healing is an outrage. When the effects of our abusive childhood have been faced, felt, known, and healed, moral guidance comes unimpeded from within. It is the right of each human being to follow that guidance exclusively.

March 1996

appendix b

Regression Therapy
in Action:
Client Case Studies
and Narratives

To give the reader an idea of why individuals had been motivated to begin this process and what their experience had been in doing it, a questionnaire was given to clients who wished to write a narrative description of what doing regressive work was like for them. A brief sketch of each client's situation is provided as well as a postscript that brings the reader up to date on what has happened since the narratives were written.

The questions asked were:

1. What was happening in your life that motivated you to seek treatment?
2. What did you know or come to know about the abuse of your childhood (the "facts")?
3. What did you know or come to know about the feelings you should have had as a child in response to that abuse?
4. What symbolic struggles were you engaged in? With whom and how did you struggle?
5. What did you have to go through to stop struggling?

6. What has it been like to feel your childhood pain?
7. How did you manage to connect your pain with childhood?
8. How has your life changed?
9. What has this process given you?
10. Under what circumstances do you think others should do it? Why?

The responses repeated here come from people in treatment for varying lengths of time. A background sketch will provide the reader with a context for the narrative, and, where appropriate, a postscript will clarify current outcome. Names and some identifying characteristics have been changed to maintain confidentiality.

ADELE

BACKGROUND: Adele was in her late twenties when she sought psychotherapy. She had been divorced for several years, having married right out of high school. Her husband was an abusive alcoholic, and the marriage did not last long. She had no children. Adele moved to a different part of the country shortly after her divorce, and it was there that her therapy began. She had no advanced education, and supported herself at first by working in various businesses that catered to the tourist trade; later she worked for the city government. She entered therapy seeking help in her relationships with men. Since divorcing her alcoholic husband, she had found that she had picked a string of men who, although not alcoholic, were as unavailable as her husband had been. When Adele entered therapy, she was tense, thin, and physically restless, punctuating almost every sentence with a high, nervous laugh. She frequently "bounced" around in her chair throughout the session, her eyes continually glancing here and there, able to engage with anyone else only briefly. Adele's family of origin consisted of herself, her parents, an older sister, and a younger brother. Her younger brother was a practicing alcoholic, and both parents drank as well; however, the family's concern about alcohol use was focused on her brother, since his drinking was totally out of control and resulted in his being hospitalized for both physical and mental problems.

Adele was not an alcoholic—in fact, she avoided drinking—but she felt an inner sense of being "out of control," and her behavior and appearance reflected that. She thought her problems were caused by her poor judgment in regard to men, and she wanted help in learning how to "make a relationship work." As we explored her childhood history and the way in which such history might be affecting her now, Adele found that she remembered very little of her childhood.

Adele's Narrative

When I started this therapy, I was in a relationship that I wanted to make work and could not. I [felt] trapped, like a failure, and unloved.

In discussing my history [of] growing up, I realized that my father was not available to me—he was always too busy. He occasionally offered some little praise for accomplishments but criticism on how I could have done the task better accompanied [it]. This I always knew, as well as the fact that he and my mother drank together every evening before dinner and during dinner. A lot of his comments [to] me were [made] during these times. My mother was quiet. She didn't seem very interested in us. It seemed to me then that Dad was more interested than Mother, just because he would talk to us sometimes, even though his criticism hurt. The other thing I began to see was that Dad also acted with sexual undercurrents toward me. I still remember very little of what actually happened, but I do remember looks, remarks, gestures, and sly smiles that were directed at me sexually and made me very uncomfortable.

When I think about how I should have felt as a child being treated this way, it seems to me I would have been hurt, but angry at him too, and at Mother for doing nothing. I think the hurt would be about being paid so little attention by either of them; and when I did get some [attention] from Dad, it was criticism. I think it would have been OK to be angry and hurt too, [at] his actions and her lack of attention.

My symbolic struggles were with men/friends who were too busy or did not appear to want to spend time with me. Sometimes I had brief relationships with men who lived in other areas or were gone most of the time. (What is interesting is my own treatment of friends in the same way! I seem to make myself unavailable also.)

When I first began to apply the principles I was learning in therapy, I could see I was doing a lot of struggling! Now that I realize (which is difficult) that I am struggling with an "old" feeling, I am getting better at acceptance of the hurt and mourning or crying with it. It's like a great wave of relief to reach this point.

My childhood pain is lonely, isolated, and never correct—a [sign of] failure. It is scary, and I feel unloved. The worst part is that, when I am feeling that old pain, it feels like it will always be this way!

It has been through the help of others working on the same problems, especially in group counseling, that I have been able to keep feeling my old pain and seeing how it connects to my child- hood. As I felt the sadness of an ended relationship and saw how hopeless it [would be] to pursue [it], I started recognizing how sim- ilar the situation was to those of my childhood where the same hopelessness and sadness existed.

I am getting to the point where I recognize "old pain" and know it won't hurt me anymore even though I allow myself to ex- perience those feelings as a part of me. I am more accepting of pain- ful feelings, knowing they will pass on and will also tell me more about what happened to me in childhood.

Although I am new at this process, it has already given me tools to live each day with, to recognize unhealthy situations and to take better care of myself. [I have also gained] the knowledge that I can call upon appropriate friends for help, [and have learned] also that I am not weird or alone in my feelings.

If other people are tired of struggling with their lives, this is a good process to use to help. Although it will bring up old fears and pain, it will give them a new view of their life. We can—with time—recognize old behaviors and choose to feel the pain of the old reality behind them without acting them out. By choosing to not re-act to situations out of our childhood feelings, but accepting the feelings these situations bring up, we are freed from unnecessary pain and fear.

POSTSCRIPT ON ADELE: After several months in therapy, Adele extricated herself from the destructive relationship in which she had felt trapped and moved to the nearest city where she could obtain a college degree. She was extremely fearful, feeling she couldn't succeed, but kept using the therapy process on her own, with supportive phone calls as necessary. Many times she felt she could not go on, could not even get out of bed, but she did, and she graduated. She returned to our community with professional employment. At this point, Adele reentered therapy because she had begun to sense that she had been sexually abused, that the sexual "overtones" from her father that she had previously recognized were only the beginning of her understanding. Although many of her original external behaviors (restlessness, reluctance to make eye contact) had abated, they were replaced by episodes of dissociation (where she would feel as if she had no life in her body) and nighttime anxiety. As she began to encounter these feelings, rather than attempt to stop them, she allowed memories of physical and sexual abuse to surface. As painful as this was, Adele was relieved to find that her present-day bizarre experiences were reasonable defensive reactions to past abuse. Adele's nervous laugh completely disappeared. Shortly after returning to therapy, she met a man and they fell in love with each other. The relationship offered Adele true intimacy (something she had unconsciously avoided), and even more painful memories emerged. Since she often symbolized on her partner, he needed help in order to understand what was happening. Her partner had no experience with such things, but he met with the therapist to discuss the problem and was willing to enter therapy himself, since he began to recognize that his own childhood history contained painful experiences that he had repressed. After a few months of "ups and downs," these two were able to effectively use their situation, growing in love for one another. They are presently planning to be married.

JACKIE

BACKGROUND: Jackie is a corporate businesswoman in her midthirties. She has never married, but is presently in a relationship with a man she likes but knows is "not long term." Jackie was in a different relationship when she entered therapy, but did not consider that to be her only problem. Jackie presented a busy, competent, efficient exterior, whether at work or at home, but described herself as "depressed," having tried different therapy solutions but not being as happy as she "should be." No matter how successful she was, she never felt accomplished or fulfilled. She has been in therapy for several years doing this regressive process, and her own narrative describes her situation very well.

Jackie's Narrative

I was in pain for a number of years to one degree or another, or just in emotional chaos. I had tried numerous self-help approaches as well as prior therapy. No matter how hard I tried to make things "right" in my life, I seemed to always fall short. Even though there were times when I enjoy[ed] myself, there seemed to always be an underlying feeling of discontent inside me.

I had literally tried everything to feel better—from therapy, self-help books, exercise, nutrition, to religion and career change. Nothing worked.

As I discovered how I was symbolizing on my relationship, and let myself feel the unhappiness [I carried] as the child I [had been] instead of trying to get rid of it, I learned that it was my mother's need to create a perfect, happy, close, loving family environment. Because of that, I acted happy. I was not able to have *any* negative feelings. I repressed them all. The only negative feeling I recall was anger, and I know now that it was a front for the pain.

All of the children in our family bought into the facade, played [their] roles and believed [that our family was a happy one]. I have found out that this was not the case.

I came to know that my sister received more than I, and it appeared to me that she was loved more, that although my role was to be strong and independent, on the inside I was just the opposite. I was a frightened, vulnerable child. I came to know that although it appeared my parents were the perfect loving partners, in reality they were not available or capable of loving me as I really was.

I came to know that I never really felt like I connected or belonged to the family in the way that they did—that my siblings were getting something more [there] than I was. I thought they were getting more love, although I know now my parents were incapable of truly loving any of us. Part of the abuse was that I wanted to "make it" like my siblings did (be "loved" like they were).

. . . I played the role of the scapegoat. I was liked least in the family. I believed I was not a good person and that I was not deserving. I felt like a failure.

Part of the abuse was that I [became] my mother's [caretaker]. I believed it was one way I could get love. I felt enmeshed with my mother. I pretended I didn't need and didn't hurt. I thought that maybe if I didn't appear needy they would find me more lovable.

In doing this work I have allowed myself to have my feelings for the first time in my life; and it amazes me how many feelings can be stored away in our bodies for years without our knowledge.

I have found that all of the childhood feelings I did not experience as a child were still inside me—and that in order to heal, I would now have to experience those feelings, for what they are (childhood feelings). These feelings can be extremely overwhelming and strong, and they often seem to be about current events, but I have come to experience that that is not true. Also, I don't just experience a feeling once, I have to revisit and feel, experience it many times in order to process it all. To feel it all at one time is impossible for me.

I have also an extreme resistance to experiencing these feelings. I used many defenses to avoid accepting these feelings. I

didn't want to believe that all this pain was actually from childhood. It has been hard for me to accept the reality and truth of
where these feelings originated. Some of my feelings are very
specific and intense, whereas other feelings are more nebulous—
feelings (Jean calls them "background feelings") were with [me]
constantly throughout [my] childhood, on a daily basis, as part of
how things were, not what was happening.

I had to learn to feel a feeling all the way through. There was
a tendency to feel it a few times and think I should be done with it.

. . . I got in touch with these feelings through current-day
events which would trigger childhood feelings and bring them to the
surface. Some of the feelings that come up are so deep and powerful
that I see now why they had to be repressed. They can be so strong,
no child could have survived experiencing them then.

The most common childhood feelings that have surfaced for
me are feelings of:

being lonely
isolated
less than, not as good as
wanting, longing, neediness
not being acknowledged
unhappy, sad
vulnerable, hurt
knowing something is missing, wrong
not being loved, wanted
a failure
not making it, missed out
emptiness
pain
not belonging, connecting
others get more
fear

In discussing symbolism, I think I could get the top prize, if
there was one. I symbolized on anything in the present. Anytime a

childhood feeling came up, I would symbolize it onto whatever situation fit that feeling today. It took me a long time to know that the feeling was really from childhood because it seemed to be so real today, to fit so perfectly. I symbolized on my boyfriend often. He brought up many feelings of having someone you love be distant, as well as not being loved and wanted. I struggled with my weight, thinking that was the problem. I also struggled with my discomfort or pain, believing it was my job, my boyfriend, the city I lived in, etc. I struggled with almost anything before me. I also struggled (symbolized) with my friends or with people at work. For example, as a child I felt like I didn't belong, so I saw myself as not belonging in regard to my coworkers.

Although I symbolized on many things, the common thread was I thought the feelings belonged to current-day events and not childhood. At times no matter how hard I tried and knew better, I couldn't help but struggle. It was as if my body could not let the information in yet. Checking in with my therapist or friends doing this work would put me back on track.

I wasted a lot of energy struggling. There was a lot of pain involved in the struggle itself. It was unnecessary pain. The only pain I needed to feel was the pain of my childhood. Finally giving in to the feelings and accepting the truth enabled me to give up the struggle. . . . It is a process. [I struggle] less and less as I become willing to let go of the illusions I had of my childhood.

The experience of feeling my childhood pain has been twofold. It is the deepest, darkest pain and despair I have ever known. Yet, it is the most wonderful feeling to connect with who I really am and [to] be free.

It took me a while to learn how to really feel. At first I tried to feel it in my head. I was disconnected with feelings and didn't know that it is a true body sensation until I began to feel both emotionally and physically. Sometimes the pain comes in the form of crying and sobbing. The sobs become deep and foreign and that of a small child. Other times feeling the pain is just walking around with it in my body as I'm working or going about my business.

Connecting my pain with childhood was also a process for me.

At first I was looking for a real strong connection, trying "too hard" to connect, and doing that kept me away from the feeling.

At first, I was trying to recall a memory, but often there were no direct memories, just sensations and feelings of the way it was. I then learned that the things I symbolized on belonged to childhood feelings and used current-day events to help make the connections when they triggered childhood feelings. Pretty soon I started to realize that most things that hurt me are about childhood. I became able to just feel whatever is there.

My life is still changing as it's only been in the last few months that I have given into this process and accepted that my unhappiness—all those feelings I listed—really [comes from] how my childhood was.

My life has changed in that I'm not depressed anymore. I may have pain now, but it's much more specific instead of a blanket feeling of depression. I feel that I do more things out of true choice, whereas before I was always driven by childhood needs. I feel more of a sense of myself, of truly being connected with me. I no longer struggle with everything. For the first time in my life I know how to feel.

When I'm not in my childhood, I just feel so happy and good inside. I never knew I could feel this way. It's peace of mind. It feels good to be alive. Everything's not an effort.

POSTSCRIPT ON JACKIE: Jackie is continuing to feel her way through to her childhood reality. Her biggest defense is her desire to believe that the picture her family painted is true, and that she can someday "get what everyone else has" through financial, employment, or relationship successes. She is currently becoming better and better at accepting the old hopelessness, and no longer needs to be a constantly busy "tryer." The moments she describes when she is "not in childhood" happen more and more often.

RAMONA

BACKGROUND: When she first entered therapy, Ramona was in her midfifties, married, with two grown daughters. Tall and stocky, with a slightly awkward posture and short, curly, tinted hair, Ramona worked as the manager of a small graphic design office; her husband ran a business. This was the first marriage for both of them, and they had been married for more than thirty years. Although Ramona had occasionally seen a counselor at times in her life when unusual events occurred, she had never undertaken ongoing psychotherapy before. Short workshops in personal growth made her think that an "uncovering" type of therapy could help her discover how her past had influenced her, as she had never felt really "OK." She tended to worry about the quality of her work, felt intimidated by both her supervisor and her employee, was overcome at times by an inexplicable sadness, and was often unreasonably angry at her husband. She tended to interfere with the life decisions of her daughters, and one was very dependent upon her. The family of her childhood consisted of a mentally ill mother, an alcoholic father, and three daughters and a son, who was the eldest. The family was poor and the house was too small, the children having to sleep in the living room. Life revolved around their mother's health (she was prone to seizures) and their father's irritability (he was prone to verbal abuse). Their brother was a favored child; the girls had to act as if they were invisible, and both parents blamed them when their mother got upset.

Ramona's Narrative

When I entered therapy my life was filled with tension. I was always angry and blamed my husband for my unhappiness. I responded to this by indulging in fantasies, especially sexual fantasies. I would always be attracted to some man in my life I imagined would rescue me from my suffering. I believed that my husband was an emotionally abusive person; this was an excuse to continually place myself in situations where I would have an affair or come dangerously close to having one. I got married because I was pregnant, and since I had spent so much of my life taking care of my agoraphobic mother, I resented having to care for a child. I remember thinking, "When was it going to be my turn to be taken care of?" I had no models for healthy parenting, and I trusted my husband to make all the decisions for our children even when I intuitively knew that they were wrong. I had low self-esteem, felt distant and alone within my marriage, and controlling with my children. My husband and I always got into fights when we went on any trip more than a few miles from home. When I was a child, my mother never went outside our home. Many times in my life I have thought that I was crazy or that I would go crazy because my mother had had two severe nervous breakdowns. Several times over the years I experienced periods of insomnia, being unable to sleep because I was so inexplicably scared. "Oh, God, I'm so scared," I remember saying to my puzzled husband. I felt different and [detached from] life as I perceived it to be for other people, and I had an extreme fear of loss. If my husband or children went somewhere out of my immediate control, I felt obsessively insecure and frightened.

Through this therapy process, I've realized that my father was an alcoholic, critical, and verbally abusive (especially to my mother) from about the time I was ten years old. My mother had low self-esteem, was very vulnerable to criticism, and exhibited extreme agoraphobia and panic attacks. Often when we children did not agree with her she would fall on the floor and have one of her "seizures" or stomp into her bedroom, where she might stay for two or three days. During this time my father would bring her meals to her. No one ever said anything about my father's drinking—although my mother, in a fit of anger, would occasionally pour his wine down the kitchen sink. I idealized my father and came to believe that we had a close relationship because we discussed politics and books. I know now that it was really a very argumentative relationship in which I believed that if I could win an intellectual argument with him I would get the affection I needed. When my father missed work or went out driving around drunk, my mother punctuated our fear and insecurity by reminding us how little money we had and by pacing the floor until our father got home. My sisters were basically ignored. My mother doted on my brother, which caused endless fights between my parents. As siblings we fought constantly. My mother's father died an alcoholic and her mother was a "crying, hysterical woman." My mother was placed in an orphanage when she was under five and was later raised by an older sister. My father's father was a heavy drinker and a stern, critical man.

I could not express my honest feelings about what was happening in my home. I experienced anger, fear, and loneliness, which went unvoiced. I feared my mother's seizures and my father's criticism, and lost trust with myself because of all the denial. I wanted to be touched and held, but this rarely happened. I kept all of this inside, where it eventually made me feel like a volcano about to explode. Since there was no way for me to check my feelings with reality, I felt like I was somehow a bad person and responsible for the family tragedy.

I am in symbolic struggles with my husband and with an employee. I have always blamed my husband for the tension in our relationship (although I secretly believed that it was all my fault because I was a bad person). In many ways my husband is unlike my father, yet he resembles him in important symbolic ways. He is sometimes very frank and insults people. He can be dominating and authoritarian. He reads books constantly and ignores me when he does. He has frequently denied my feelings and seems to want to pursue an intellectual argument over the slightest comment. I have reacted to this by swallowing my feelings, constantly blaming, and trying to get a lot of physical and mental space from him. My employee is a woman much like my mother. She has areas of low self-esteem and her feelings are hurt easily. If I confront her about something, she threatens to run out of the office (and she has). I have reacted to this by tiptoeing around her and taking great care not to disagree with her. She is gossipy and wants to know everything about me. She listens in on my phone calls. My mother violated my boundaries by listening to my phone calls and snooping around when I was doing anything by myself. As a result I have become very secretive around my employee; and because she makes me feel like I'm suffocating, I create a lot of physical and mental space between us. My husband has two male friends whom I despise (they have been alcoholics most of their adult lives) because they remind me of my father, and I have a couple of female friends with whom I have the same boundary problems as I have with my mother/employee.

To stop struggling, I have first had to recognize the struggles at face value. Then I have had to train myself over and over to recognize when I am in a symbolic struggle: "This is a childhood feeling," I have to say to myself. "This situation does not warrant this particular reaction." Then I allow myself to feel the sensations in my body and just stay with them at that moment. I have had to force myself to say things to my husband that I had been afraid to say because I believed that he would yell at me or, worse yet, leave me. I have had to say things to my employee that I avoided saying because I was afraid that she would have a seizure (like my mother) or run out of the room. I have had to grieve for my lost childhood and have cried so much at times that I have wondered if this therapy might be harmful. But so far the end result has been beneficial.

When I confront my symbolic struggles, I am sometimes overwhelmed by powerful feelings like fear, nausea, and craziness, but I feel much stronger and better afterwards. It is like feeling you are going to die from it and then surviving and having a better life because of it. It is frightening [for me] to speak to my husband when I think he might be angry or abandon me. It is equally so when I confront my employee when I think she might run out of the room or have a seizure, but I do it.

I have been able to connect my pain to childhood by having slowly recollected specific incidents from my childhood which made me feel the same way I feel in the presence of my husband or employee. I felt scared and insecure when my mother paced the floor waiting for my father to come home from his nighttime driving forays. What if he left us forever? I felt angry when he insulted my friends with his alcoholic boasting. I felt overwhelmed with fear when my mother would thrash around on the floor during one of her seizures. I felt suffocated by my mother's constant presence and by my lack of privacy in what was really a one-bedroom house where we children slept in the living room. Since I usually took my father's side in family disagreements, my mother's vulnerability made me feel like I was a bad person.

Recent examples of situations that were symbolic to me:

- My husband wanted to go to a movie the other night, but I said that it was a movie I didn't want to see. So he decided to go alone. At first I felt abandoned, and almost went so that I didn't have to feel the loss. Instead, I stayed home and just stayed with my feelings.
- I had to be very forthright about something with an old friend. When she didn't call me for a couple of weeks, I wanted to call her and reassure myself that she still liked me. Instead, I felt those feelings of being a bad person and needing to be liked, and I didn't call until I was clear of those.
- Today I wasn't able to get the new person at work to understand how to size a picture for the new schedule. When I felt myself going into a rage over this I realized that these were old feelings about not being able to get through to my parents. I had to stay with this feeling all day before I was in an adult state again.
- A friend said that she would call me around one o'clock about going for a walk. By two o'clock I thought that she was either afraid to call me and tell me she changed her mind or that I didn't have any value, so why should she call? So I left for a walk by myself. When I got back, I called her and told her what had happened and that this had brought up some old feelings and asked her if she had been afraid to call. She said that she had been delayed in town and had called me around two o'clock, but that I was gone. She assured me that if she had changed her mind she would have let me know. She thanked me for talking to her about it. I knew if I hadn't, I would carry the resentment for a long time and it would affect the relationship.
- A friend in Portland called, and, as usual, was feeling bad about herself. She wasn't doing any art work. She was fat. She was be-

hind in painting a mural she'd been commissioned to do. She had spent too much money. She wasn't getting any exercise. She was taking on too many projects—the usual litany. I like this person and she is very talented, but I no longer feel as though I have to rescue my friends or my children. So I just listened and employed techniques we have used in group to let someone know we care, but refrained from rushing in to solve her problems.

- My employee started asking me about something quasi-confidential that had to do with my husband's job in the public sector. I started to discuss it, and then realized how uncomfortable I felt. The phone rang at that moment so I left to do some work in the print shop. When I got there I realized that I needed to tell my employee that I wasn't prepared to talk about the subject, but would attempt to do so later if she asked again. We all got busy and she didn't ask again, but I didn't bring it up either. In the past, I would have made an opening to continue the subject so that she would like and approve of me.

The way my life has changed so far is, first, there is less tension, anger, and depression in my life. I seldom have problems with sleep. I feel closer to people—more on the inside of the social world than on the outside, looking in. There are fewer occasions when I feel like a six-year-old talking to adults and longing to know what to say. I trust my intuition more and make better decisions for myself. My youngest daughter (age twenty-three) and I have become close friends after her contentious, angry childhood. I have stopped rescuing my oldest daughter (age twenty-five) and a more honest, trusting, and caring relationship is beginning to develop between us. About eighty percent of the time I can stop struggling with my husband when I see we are headed for an intellectual argument over "who is right." Our relationship is improving, although I sometimes still get caught up in episodes of blaming. I can go beyond my childhood fears more often and say and do the things I want to say and do.

This process, which I have combined with a Vipassana meditation practice, has given me more inner space than I ever thought I would have in this life. I know now that I was not responsible for my family history and I am beginning to believe that I am actually a good person to whom good things can happen.

This method can be good for people because it doesn't require medication and doesn't promise instant relief or claim that one can get their childhood needs met now. It provides tools one can apply throughout one's life, especially after leaving the security of therapy. And more importantly, it is a method easily understood by the average person and not confused by excessive psychological jargon or requiring dependence on a therapist-guru. Knowing what I know now (from my experience), I don't believe that anyone with a family history similar to mine could make any significant progress without understanding their childhood, no matter how painful.

POSTSCRIPT TO RAMONA: Ramona has continued to use the regressive process in her life independently, coming in for only an occasional therapy session. As a result of the therapy, she was able to make the decision to leave the supposed financial security of her job (her husband can support her, if necessary) and engage in freelance design work, her lifelong dream. To do this, she not only had to be willing to depend on her husband, overcoming her symbolic belief that he was not available for this, but also to "give up on" attempting to mollify her touchy employee. As her narrative shows, her life has improved in many specific ways.

DANA

BACKGROUND: Dana was in her midthirties when she started this psychotherapy method and had been using it for several months when responding to this questionnaire. Although she is a college-educated woman, she worked as a tour guide in the summer and landscaper in the winter in order to live in our mountain resort community. Dana's father was a practicing alcoholic and her mother enabled his drinking, offering the children no protection from his verbal, physical, and sexual abuse. Dana had very few specific memories of

childhood when entering therapy. She had attended AA and ACA
for several months but felt she was not able to make significant
changes through those programs. She was overweight and unhappy
about that, as well as many other things in her life. She was very
verbal and expressed herself easily, but tended to focus on little
things people had done during her week that bothered her, almost always finding herself in a position of being helplessly victimized.
When describing the situations, Dana tended to tell them as "funny
stories," laughing at them herself.

Dana's Narrative

I sought psychotherapy for several reasons. I had low self-esteem. I
didn't think I was good enough. I was angry and difficult to get
along with. I was very whiny. My finances were a mess. I had difficulty taking care of myself and paying bills. I would push friends
away with sarcasm and anger. I was going to AA meetings and
hated a lot of the men there and judged them. I had unhealthy relationships with men—emotionally unavailable men who reinforced
my bad feelings about myself. They were usually alcoholic and sexually unavailable. I was tired of going to AA and ACA (Adult Children of Alcoholics) meetings and not getting anywhere. I also went
to a lot of private therapists and group therapies and still felt I had
not made any progress with my problems.

I had almost no memories when entering therapy, and now I
have some of the picture. I know this much so far: My father severely pounded on me verbally. He would dump his anger or
worldviews on me. He overreacted emotionally at me. He drank and
became very inconsistent when drinking. He yelled a lot and was
grandiose. My father was belligerent at the dinner table and made
meals "hell." My mother never stood up for me against my father,
letting him also spank me, tease me unmercifully, and belittle me. I
am also quite sure I was sexually abused, because I have most of the
symptoms of a sexually abused person. At this time I have no specific memories. I have also become aware that my father decided
everything and no one else in the family was given any choices.

Through the therapy I have so far come to know that nobody cared enough about me to do anything to help. No one loved me. I felt "How could they not care?" and "How could they do something like that?" I felt lonely and alone, hopeless and scared. I felt "How unfair!" I felt the need for it to be OK to cry and to cry for a long time.

I see now that I have created similar environments in my life— [relationships with people who] will treat me as if they don't care, [relationships that] bring me the feelings of how unfair it [all] was and how lonely, hopeless and [uncared for] I felt. I symbolize on both work and relationships in this way. With regard to work: I pick incredibly unfair bosses, who are often asking the impossible, and then I want them to care and be fair and reasonable and to treat me with kindness. Relationships: I choose emotionally and sexually unavailable men, and then I struggle to be a good girl so they'll love me. For these men, I could not be enough. With roommates and friends: I pick ones who I don't relate closely with and I feel like I have to defend myself. They don't follow through on plans made. They say one thing and do another. Also, I have no safe place to live. (I haven't enough money to rent a decent place for myself alone, so I always need roommates, and, during the summer when I [am a] horse pack guide, I have to share quarters with people [whom] I don't know well and who drink a lot.)

In order to stop struggling, I stick to the facts at hand, I listen for "key statements," and I use my anger as a clue. I know that when I'm angry, I am usually hurt underneath it and am in a struggle with someone. Once the clues alert me to the struggle, I repeat "This is old" until I believe it and connect the old childhood truth to the feeling that is making me react in the present situation. Then I feel the old feelings and pain. Afterwards, the person or situation I'm struggling with is put into perspective for the job at hand. I also try to let go of people, places, and things that don't fit a healthier life.

The pain from my childhood feels like it would have back then if I would have been able to allow it to happen then. It's important for me to give myself a safe place to have and express my feelings because that wasn't available in the past. It is very scary—

physically and emotionally draining. I have found for myself that I stored these unfelt feelings in different parts of my body. So when I would experience the pain I would have energy move through my body, i.e., tingling sensations in my legs, throbbing in my sides, etc. Once I felt so much pain that the energy released through the top of my head made my scalp feel very bruised for three days.

One thing I learned was to stop interrupting my crying to blow my nose. When I did that, it took me out of my old feeling, and I wanted to mention it here because someone might be doing that too.

I am finding that as I let go of the struggle and pain, I have found more room in my life for joy and serenity. I have a spiritual program I can use and am able to choose healthier relationships with jobs and friends. I make more right decisions for myself. I am more of an adult and am able to take care of myself better.

I feel very different about myself in a positive way (feelings). I have personal integrity, more freedom of choice. My life is mine, and this process gives me tools to use to continue to move forward. I am able to believe my intuitions now.

I encourage everyone to find the courage to go through this process one step at a time. You can't get beyond the problems you have that were caused by childhood abuse until you go through it. It works for me, and it's worth it.

POSTSCRIPT ON DANA: Some aspects of Dana's life have changed considerably. She has continued in therapy, with some "breaks" of several weeks at a time. At this time, she is no longer a seasonal tour guide, but working full-time in the resort business. She is supporting herself adequately, and has purchased a new home through an FHA loan. She is confronting problems with work or friends as they arise, no longer feeling like a helpless victim. At times she feels very lonely, and lets herself feel how lonely her childhood was. Also, she is still in a lot of pain about her weight, currently feeling the wish to "have a different body." When describing her current experiences, she seldom presents them as "funny stories," and it is apparent now that both her laughter and her anger are clues to underlying hurt. She has begun to experience specific abuse memories as well.

SARAH

BACKGROUND: When she entered therapy, Sarah was in her early thirties, single, and supporting herself in a service industry. She had lived several hundred miles away from her family of origin for many years and had little contact with them. She had two older brothers and no sisters. Her mother was absent emotionally and physically, often "sick" in her bedroom for days on end. Sarah's father and brothers were verbally and physically abusive to her, with her mother providing her no protection. She would often come home from school to find nothing but the closed door of her mother's door to greet her. In her teens, she began to use drugs supplied by her brothers. She was a recovering alcoholic and drug addict upon entering treatment. Sarah wanted to have a healthy relationship with a man, something that had not yet happened to her.

Sarah's Narrative

The reason I sought treatment is that I kept getting into relationships which usually ended quickly and left me feeling bad about myself.

Regarding the men I spent time with, my friends would frequently comment, "You can do so much better—I don't know what you see in him."

I began to suspect that some of these "patterns" I was hearing about were operating in my life, since all of my relationships with men ended in painful disappointment. And I began to suspect the problem was inside me and thought I might be able to discover this in therapy.

In this therapy, I learned that my needs (as a child) had not [been] met, that the neglect from my family—in particular, my mother—was abuse.

The nature of my abuse was partly due to my mother's drinking, which left her incapacitated.

I was not loved or disciplined. I was not allowed to show feelings, communicate, ask for things, explore. I was punished for taking care of myself. One example: At about age fourteen I was hungry and ate a piece of pie in the refrigerator. My father scolded me, telling me it was the last piece and he had been saving it for himself. (He was an overeater.) I felt terrible.

My brothers were older. The oldest brother held me down and tickled me torturously, called me a "spoiled brat" almost daily, and gave me "speed" when I was a teenager.

I know now that to show my feelings brought punishment so I learned to numb myself. Those feelings came out in unhealthy expressions such as frequent picking at myself, my skin and hair. I learned not to cry or feel anger, and I frequently made myself physically sick with headaches, stomachaches, chest pains, hyperventilation, insomnia, and sugar addiction.

At the age of five or six I was hospitalized for three weeks and put under observation and testing to determine the cause of these illnesses. I was released with no finding of anything wrong. It is my belief I was an angry, frightened, neglected child who "worried herself sick."

Growing up, I frequently was overpowered by my father and my two older brothers. Today I struggle with asserting myself when facing situations involving my boyfriend and his two sons. The duplication of facing three males causes me to struggle between submission and healthy assertiveness.

In my family, no one ever told me everything, or the "whole story." As a child I had to fill in a lot of the missing information so I would "overthink," "underfeel," and stay confused and out of touch. I tend to re-create these struggles in everyday life. Today I tend to "read between the lines" a lot instead of listening directly and to complicate the incoming message with my own thoughts in an effort to figure things out, which only causes additional interference.

I am having to recognize patterns, such as choosing unavailable men and creating fantasy relationships, then acting as if they're real and when the results [I want] don't come, experiencing disappointment and blaming them.

I had to stop being with these men, which left me without the company of men, at least sexually, until some sort of transition could be made.

I also had to stop drinking to begin to use my senses in making healthier choices with men.

Feeling my childhood pain has been uncomfortable. From slight muscle tension to severe psychosomatic illness, it has been very physical for me. Recently it has been more emotional. The physical symptoms include hyperventilation, chest pains, nausea, headache, dry heaving, sweating, chilling, shaking, loss or gain of appetite, lethargy, hyperkinesis.

Emotionally, I have had extreme episodes of crying, feeling afraid, sad, and worrying.

I have experienced insomnia.

Example: I went to an AA meeting and saw my boyfriend's (then) wife. I became tense, and had difficulty breathing. Next I felt chest pains followed by nausea while driving home in my car. I had to leave the meeting before it ended as I was feeling "ill." While driving home from the meeting in my car I had considered driving myself to the local hospital emergency room for chest pains and requesting some tranquilizers, but since I'm a recovering addict, I decided against it, and instead brought it to therapy. Feeling it in therapy revealed to me that I was reacting with my childhood fear of my own mother's (now deceased) anger. This situation had duplicated the reactions for which my parents had hospitalized me, when the doctors found nothing wrong.

My friends [told me] that my behavior [showed] a pattern of creating painful situations, and I spent a lot of time being very unhappy with the way my life was going.

I heard that by recognizing these patterns I might be able to find ways to change them through making healthier choices, but first I had to identify the pain within the pattern and discover what I was doing to keep the pain in place.

I began to "trace" my present pain back through past memories to my very first recollection of the pain. Then I would "re-feel" the pain in its former original context and "connect" it to the present pain and realize they were matched. I would look for elements in my present painful situation and discover the pattern.

Many of my struggles today match my childhood struggles.

I was raised by a mother, father, and two older brothers. I am marrying a man with two sons and an ex-wife.

I get/got angry at my fiancé's/father's inability to feel. I become/became afraid of my fiancé's ex-wife's/my mother's anger; I symbolize on my fiancé as being my father and his ex-wife as my mother.

When my fiancé, his sons, and I are together, I feel very small and overpowered, like when I was with Dad and older brothers.

My life has changed drastically [since starting this therapy].

By tolerating the discomforts of my childhood pain, I have been able to stay clean and sober for almost three years. I can feel and continue to experience deeper levels of feeling.

I have moved from isolation through living alone for eleven years to becoming engaged to marry a man with children.

I have gone back to school and completed twenty-five percent of a master's degree with straight A's. I have not missed any work due to illness or otherwise.

I continue to find greater happiness and satisfaction in my life.

This process has given me tools and techniques which I believe are keeping me alive and healthy.

I have learned to separate the present from the past and have gained control over old, self-destructive habits. I have learned a way to end the sabotage through engaging in relationships of success in my life. I can now think before I react inappropriately. I found a path to self-acceptance.

The process has given me self-confidence, compassion, courage, happiness, and physical health. I think others could benefit from this therapy, and I would wish for anyone's life to change as positively as I believe mine has. I keep getting better. My bad days are fewer and farther between. It works for me.

POSTSCRIPT ON SARAH: The man Sarah married turned out to be unavailable also (although in a way different from what she was used to) and Sarah used her therapy process to help her through the heart-ache of that. She was able to grieve the deep disappointment of the present and the old emotional abandonment of her childhood that this experience brought up to her. She gained the strength to reorganize her life according to her own needs, and let go of the relationship. She is currently single.

MARTHA

BACKGROUND: Martha is a married woman with two young adolescent boys. Martha's husband is a successful businessman and she is able to be a full-time mother. She is a college-educated woman and serves on local boards and engages in developing community services designed to help meet social needs of the adolescent population. Martha entered treatment because she felt unfulfilled in some way despite her successful community work. She had attended a lecture on co-dependency, felt that much of it applied to her, and decided that perhaps some therapy would help.

Martha's Narrative

I was motivated to begin therapy because I was in midlife malaise—overworked, underloved—asking, "Is this all there is?" I wanted to move from mere survival to flourishing. I had heard Jean speak on an earlier occasion, but I really "heard" her in December of 1990. Every description of co-dependency fit me! I did not want a class, since I know I escape to my intellect so easily, and I did not want to share her in a group, so I chose individual therapy.

I had known facts about my childhood for a long time. Therapy helped me realize the implications of [what I knew]. My father was away at World War II for the first two years of my life. I was born when my mother was thirty-six, and I was the first child. My father was an alcoholic—the perennial college-fraternity-boy type. My mother had expected my father to become a college professor, with suede-patched tweed jacket and pipe and university life. Instead, he became an underpaid high school language teacher. My mother was the worrier, the financial organizer, and a depressed and isolated woman. These situations resulted in my being neglected by both parents with regard to emotional nurturing. They were incapable and unconscious.

In response to my childhood neglect and abandonment I chose to become strong, denied my need/feelings in deference to [those of] my mother, and took on the task of making her happy. I should have responded with hurt and anger, but those feelings would have annihilated me then.

I have been in symbolic struggles with males in my life in an attempt to command attention and get affection. I chose my spouse to struggle with for twenty-three years. He has a pattern of withdrawing in silence when he is angry—as my mother did. I have also used my work as a symbolic struggle to achieve a "connection" that I never had in my family of origin. My work consists of creating highly charged emotional experiences [for] younger people who would then "love" me.

To stop my struggling I needed to remind myself that all I long for is *old* need. The sense of longing is my cue to help me take the charge out of present-day love/work situations. I remember, "Something this intense is *old*." I then go back (connect mentally and emotionally) to the original scenario and allow myself to feel the neglect, abandonment, and lack of connection that I needed "then." I resisted this childhood pain; at first I was able to feel it in the safety of Jean's presence only. I felt it in my physical body—a real surprise to me—and I feel it especially in my belly—a knot of fear. I have noticed that as I am feeling these "negative" painful feelings more, I am also more able to feel pleasurable emotions and physical sexual feelings. I am regaining a range of feelings I once chose to shut down.

On many occasions when my feelings are connected to childhood, I have felt very young, seen inner images of [myself] crying, unattended in a crib. Sometimes I see my childhood home through the eyes of a child—my perspective is that of a young child. Rationally I know the feelings are not linked to my present, adult abilities, but rather they are nonrational, from another state of consciousness.

Each time I go through an episode of feeling old pain, I reassure myself that I am an adult now and am able to survive that pain. The only way out is through!

My life has changed, as I am now able to catch when childhood pain is triggered and allow myself to feel that pain (at the moment or when appropriate) and not escape into rationalizations ("My childhood wasn't so bad," "What's the big deal?," "The other's needs are more important than mine," etc.).

I can recognize more quickly my slipping into old hope and euphoria—my voice goes up and words come rapidly, churning up that old hope and enthusiasm to keep Mommy happy. I am not panicked about tomorrow—[a] relationship is not the end-all to life. I am not attached to outcome in my work. I notice when intensity is sought by my childhood state of consciousness and allow underlying feelings to be felt. I *feel*! That's the greatest change. I once believed I was only my head—there was no sensation below neck level. I [now] surrender and allow feeling.

This process has given me awareness, choice in my behavior, and tools with which to deal with my pain.

I wholeheartedly recommend this process to others as it brings joy, confidence, concrete techniques for living life in stereophonic feeling—with passion!

MARTHA'S POSTSCRIPT ON HERSELF: Three years after therapy I have fewer occasions to feel old pain. I still don't like it, but I allow myself the experience knowing I will get through it and "feel" better. I continue to use what Jean taught me to deepen my self-knowledge and personal growth.

ADDITIONAL POSTSCRIPT: Martha has continued to contribute to the well-being of the community in this way. However, she no longer attempts to use those contributions to fill her childhood needs.

LENNY

BACKGROUND: Lenny is married to his second wife, who has been in therapy for a long time. Lenny has had an intellectual understanding of the concepts because of that, but was not motivated to come into therapy himself until his wife fell in love with another man. The situation was open and aboveboard, in that Lenny and his wife discussed it together; and he, seeing himself as an "evolved person," gave her permission to have an affair. However, he had much more difficulty than he had anticipated in accepting the situation and decided to get help.

Lenny's Narrative

My wife was with another lover—a situation which was throwing me into much confusion, anger, and (old) pain. Also, she was doing her own therapy work and I was learning from her insights.

Prior to therapy I had not known that, as a child, I was physically abused by jerking, slapping, and spanking, emotionally abused by abandonment and guilt trips, and emotionally/sexually abused by my mother, who used my presence as a substitute for her alcoholic husband.

Neither of my parents could deal with anything troublesome from their children, so I sat on feelings of being unlovable and unwanted with the hurt and pain that cooked up. I was not allowed to express anger, either.

I have always reacted symbolically to my wife. I wanted to pull away from her as a knee-jerk response to feeling hurt. I was addicted to her love in an unconscious attempt to get [the] genuine love from my mother which I didn't [get] as a child.

[In order to stop struggling,] I had to get understanding (about how I felt and what I was doing to cover it up), then express anger (which always came first), and then the pent-up hurt and pain. I had to consciously recognize my desire to pull away from my wife and open up to her instead, and tell her how I was feeling.

It has been hard to look at my feelings honestly and feel the pain, but it helps so much!

To connect my feelings with childhood, I tried to feel what I was feeling in the present, then just close my eyes and let my focus gradually move down the path to childhood.

By doing this, the huge "wound" that I was carrying feels healed to a great degree. I feel whole and empowered for the first time in my life!!

This process has given me myself—and what else is there? I'm now able to bring a more real me to my marriage.

For me, the therapy has been the key to releasing many of the unconscious drives that could have ruined my life. You can never be whole or free if a part of you is stuck in the past, trying to get something you can never get.

POSTSCRIPT ON LENNY: Lenny and his wife have continued to work on their relationship problems by each of them recognizing when they are symbolizing and using it to uncover more of the painful memories of their childhoods. Lenny has become good at opening up instead of withdrawing. The affair is long over, Lenny having realized that he needed to take the stand that his wife had to choose between him and her lover. For her, there was no comparison, and the choice was easily Lenny. A new emotional and sexual intimacy has developed between them, facilitated by both this experience and the therapy work.

NADINE

BACKGROUND: Nadine is a woman in her midtwenties, engaged to a man a few years older. They had been living together for some time, but had separated at the time she sought therapy. Nadine and her fiancé were having terrible shouting matches, with one or both of them breaking down emotionally. Neither of them could understand why this kept happening, and the issues seemed to be unimportant. They knew they could not marry without solving this problem.

Nadine was pessimistic about their chances, and was the one to move out, but she wanted to make a final effort through therapy.

Nadine's Narrative

I entered therapy because I was involved in a relationship which I wanted to continue, yet [which] seemed to be falling apart, beyond my control.

As I examined my childhood for experiences that could shed light on the problems my fiancé and I were having, I learned that neither of my parents was available for me, my mother being an alcoholic, my father a workaholic. Both cared more about their own lives than their children. My brothers, one in particular, were physically abusive. The memories had been completely blocked.

I have come to realize that the feelings I should have had in response to that abuse were buried or changed to "safer" feelings (i.e., anger or rage changed to feelings of guilt).

Some of the ways I symbolize are unrelated to people, and have more to do with situations. For instance, I have had a lot of fear that someone is going to "chop me up," usually when I am home, or on a walk, alone. This is symbolic of my abusive brothers. They beat me up as a child.

I struggle with emotions of rage whenever someone is late to meet me. I see now that it is my childhood rage because of a mother who was late by hours while I waited someplace for her.

Whenever my fiancé loses his temper I become terrified. This is symbolic of the situation when my brother came after me when he became mad and physically abused me.

When my fiancé does not believe me about something I become so angry. [As I was] growing up, my parents never believed me when I told them that one of my brothers had physically abused me. They believed that I broke my glasses, not that my brother hit me in the face and broke them.

I used to imagine dead bodies on the other side of any unopened door [and was] always afraid of opening that door. My mother often threatened to commit suicide over the phone, then hung up and wouldn't answer when I tried to call back. Whenever I came home I expected her to be dead.

Now I am able, a lot of the time, to see or feel when I am struggling. I try to let go and feel the pain, knowing it is from childhood. Often I still do not know what is triggering me or what happened to go with the feelings in childhood, but I am aware of the struggle and can feel an old pain.

For example, once I was standing between a window and a bed, watering some plants. I had a familiar feeling that someone bad was under the bed that was going to grab my ankle, pull me down, and chop me up. I used to get down on my hands and knees to check under the bed, but this time I felt the fear, knowing that the fear, the feelings, were childhood. The reality, I knew this time, was that no one was under the bed.

Another example: A woman I work with really dislikes me. There is no apparent reason. I used to try so hard to change her feelings for me, to make her like me. The other day I felt the pain and wanted to do something to change it, but only for a moment. Instead, I felt that old pain of people who didn't like me because of my strange drug/alcoholic family.

My body hurts when I feel the childhood pain. Usually my stomach and oftentimes my head feels like it will explode with pressure. My heart aches. After feeling the pain for some time I feel drained.

I managed to connect the pain with childhood through the therapy. I am learning that that much pain must be childhood pain.

My life has changed very much. I understand that my fears are [from] childhood, so I don't spend my days feeling a fear is realistic—that someone will chop me up at any moment.

When I realize I am struggling with my fiancé, I stop fighting. Our house is so much quieter. Instead of spending a Saturday arguing, we go for a hike and have fun!

I no longer feel the need to be verbally abusive to those around me. I realize my anger is in me, it is [from] childhood, [that those around me now] didn't do something to me.

This process has given me peace, hope, and understanding. It has given me a much better life, a happy life.

I think everyone who struggles should do this. I feel it is necessary for people to understand why they struggle. Through understanding, people may want to grow more. We would have healthier people in this world, healthier children.

POSTSCRIPT ON NADINE: Nadine and her fiancé married about one and a half years after Nadine entered therapy. Her fiancé began therapy, too, and they entered couples therapy when they got stuck in symbolic responses to one another. They have built their own house together since the time Nadine's narrative was written, and they have just had their second child. They get along well most of the time and call for help when they need it.

BETTY

BACKGROUND: Betty was in her early thirties when she came into therapy. She was hoping to figure out why she was in a relationship that was so rejecting of her. Betty is a college-educated woman. A few years following college graduation, Betty had moved far away from home, and now made "duty" visits to her parents, often returning with stories of how difficult their relationship was. She was very conflicted about her relationship with her boyfriend, and was living with him in a new home he had built at the time she entered treatment. She had sought graduate education and was working as a paralegal, something in which her boyfriend had a big stake. This was another area of conflict, as this was not the employment Betty would have chosen for herself, either with regard to the type of work or the hours spent. She really wanted something that gave her more time than money, but her boyfriend felt strongly that she would not be fully contributing to their situation if she changed her job. Because of this conflict and ways in which she felt she was being abused verbally, Betty thought she should move but was terrified of the feelings that she might have to face if she lived alone.

Betty's Narrative

I was motivated to seek therapy [because] I was living with my boy-friend and beginning to feel the same way I had felt when I was married (seven years earlier) whenever my boyfriend and I would have a fight. The two men seemed very different to me; thus, I felt it must have to do with me.

Exploring my childhood confirmed the sense that I had always had—that my father was critical and physically abusive. He also put me down as a girl, making snide references to the size of my feet, hips, etc. My mother would plead with him (usually at the dinner ta-ble) to stop. She would take my side for a while, then shift to his side and lash out at me, telling me what a good man [my father] was.

I discovered that, as a child, I had feelings of extreme loneli-ness, abandonment, excessive desire to make people like me, [which led] to my wanting abusive boyfriends to be kind to me to avoid dealing with the awful pain that my father's [criticism had left me with].

I am still struggling with Tom, my "boyfriend"—he doesn't *like* me—[and] that's so compelling for me that I find myself trying to get him to like me from time to time. I also can't accept that he just plain old doesn't—a total replay of my relationship with Dad.

In order to stop struggling, I have to tell myself, "Hold still and just feel." Usually the feelings are gut-ripping painful. My second rule was "Don't call Tom."

The best way I can describe what feeling old pain is like is a vast open space filled with dark whirling nothingness that goes on forever. The pain in this space feels as though it will kill me.

My first connection where I knew that feelings I had were re-ally from childhood came with three abandoned kittens I found at a roadside rest area a few years ago. The pain I felt at leaving them there connected to three kittens I had to leave at the pound years ago. It was horrible to drive off (with my father) and leave them. I knew they would die, but I had no way to get to feel my feelings about this.

My life has changed in that I am making more and more conscious decisions to put myself around people who like me. I am consciously taking care of myself—watching out for what is good for me [rather than just] not taking care of others. Day by day it gets clearer.

This process has given me a lifelong commitment to working toward clarity—a commitment to myself and a sense of myself and what I am. I don't have to apologize any longer. (The strength comes and goes, but at least I feel it growing!)

I think anyone would benefit from this process, and that if it is right for them to do so, the time will also come for them to do it.

POSTSCRIPT ON BETTY: Shortly after entering therapy, Betty decided to move out of her boyfriend's house, and, to help with her feelings of being alone, she moved in with another woman. After a while, she found her own place and has lived alone since, although for many months she and her boyfriend would get back together and break up again, over and over. She never moved back in with him, however, and eventually broke up with him for good. She is single at this time. In terms of her work, Betty found more satisfying part-time employment, taking on responsibility for a local community service organization. This meets her needs for both challenge and time to engage in other activities. Betty also became clear about her difficulties with the visits to her parents; she realizes that her father is still abusive, but she doesn't need him to be nice to her now, as an adult. She is able to overlook his comments and take satisfaction in the visit simply because they are her parents.

SHERYL

BACKGROUND: Sheryl was a young woman in her early twenties, a recovering drug addict and alcoholic, who was overweight and smoked when she entered therapy. She had two congenital physical problems—a "wandering eye" and some serious dental problems that needed correcting. All of these factors made her feel very unattractive. Sheryl had been "using" since high school, so her only academic achievement was to graduate. She has no advanced schooling and had been fired from an airline job because of her drug use. She was irresponsible with money and worked at a low-paying job, something about which she complained a lot. She seemed to be hoping someone else would take care of her (as her parents should have). Sheryl's relationship with her father was difficult for her, in that he and her mother were divorced and he had remarried, and neither her father nor his new wife seemed to care about her and her problems, something that was true since childhood. Her mother was a practicing alcoholic who had remarried, to a man who sexually abused Sheryl for years. Her mother was still drinking and Sheryl was constantly trying to get her to "see the light." At the beginning of therapy, she still had a lot of unreal hope attached to both parents. However, she was usually motivated to deal with all of her problems, despite the fact that she had not been sober for more than a few weeks. She knew that her addictions did not end with drugs and alcohol and that she could not make her life better without overcoming all of them.

Sheryl's Narrative

I had a history of incest. I was trying an after-care group and didn't feel I was getting anywhere. Several women from ISA (Incest Survivors Anonymous) mentioned Jean's name a lot and recommended her as a therapist.

After working a while in therapy, I learned that I hadn't been taken care of, physically, emotionally, and spiritually. My needs were not met. Sometimes denial, which I've discovered is very powerful, still sneaks up on me. But I've learned enough from therapy to not minimize my experience.

Before therapy, I thought the feelings that turned out to be from my childhood were adult feelings. Now I can take it back to the abuse. I often feel totally alone and isolated because I was abandoned then, for example. Or fear—it was too scary to feel it as a child, I wasn't allowed to, I had to be the adult, had to take care of their feelings.

I have struggles with men and authority figures. I depend on men to get old needs met—i.e., affection, security, to feel needed and loved. I can't (won't) stand up to authority figures today. I give them too much power and I'm afraid. When they have control I feel powerless. I feel "less than."

[In order to stop struggling,] I've had to use a "reality check" (asking someone if my feelings make present sense), and find the courage to stand up for myself regardless of right/wrong or consequences. With men, I've had to do SA (Sex Addicts Anonymous) and make a commitment to celibacy, so I don't try to get something from them that I'll never get. The reason for this is that I always go after men who are not interested in me, as symbolic for the lack of interest my parents had in me. Only by committing to celibacy have I been able to contain myself, but it's been really hard, because if I don't ask a man out, no one asks me, so I either do things with girlfriends or stay home alone. It makes me feel very deprived and I try to let that happen.

The worst, most intense feelings I have feel like "the end" (death). This is terrible. I feel alone and worthless a lot too, but after each experience with the pain I feel growth and relief, [and less] hopeless.

In order to connect my painful feelings with childhood, again, I do a "reality check." If I'm reacting with intense feelings over normal adult stuff, I know it's childhood. I usually have to talk about it with someone who has perspective on their childhood stuff before I can identify what I'm feeling. I don't usually go to a certain incident. Thinking too much takes me out of the pain.

It is hard for me to describe how I have changed. I *know* I've changed, but I don't feel it very often because I'm in childhood feelings so much. I don't always react to anger today, and I go through uncomfortable situations instead of ignoring them or running. I tell my parents how I feel about things, I stand up to them now. I feel responsible for my life and take care of myself physically, but I'm working on the emotional and spiritual.

This process has given me real hope.

I think feeling the pain now that you didn't feel then could be a good process for everyone. Not the "child within" crap. That shit just brings up shame and gets you out of the feeling (which isn't how I felt about it a few months ago). As I said before, denial is powerful and I'll do anything to get out of the pain. That's why I'm cross-addicted.

POSTSCRIPT ON SHERYL: Sheryl's narrative was written three years ago. She stayed in weekly therapy until a few months ago, when she left her low-paying job to move to a city where she could go to school and find employment that would support her while doing so. During her time in therapy, Sheryl had corrective eye and mouth surgery, as well as orthodontic work. She improved her appearance considerably, but had no success in losing weight or in feeling better about her weight. She was able to accept the reality that her appearance had improved regardless of her weight. She was able to maintain her sobriety and quit smoking, but was unable to stay "sober" with regard to her celibacy commitment. She is still struggling with her desire to chase unavailable men. Before leaving therapy here, Sheryl confronted her father about his current uncaring, neglectful treatment of her, expecting nothing as a result, but knowing that she had not allowed the abuse of her childhood to continue now by keeping silent. She has been able to relate to her mother without trying to "fix" her alcoholism. Sheryl's move to the city and eventually to go to school is a very healthy plan for her to take care of herself, instead of symbolically hoping someone else will.

I received the following, quite unsolicited letter from a friend of a former client who had done everything she could to teach him the regressive process:

My motivation for as long as I can remember, for just about everything I have ever done, has been to stop the pain I feel.

I think I have been stuck in the same emotional/

psychological mind-set for a long time. What I have learned about the nature of the work to be done, I have learned by process of elimination. In other words, what I have done so far hasn't worked. And so far, I think I have done a lot.

I believe now that I cannot act my way out of the place I am in. I have acted well. I have done all the things I could think of to do that were good for me. I have prayed and meditated. I have exercised and eaten well. I have been an honest and valuable employee and given an honest day's work for my wages. I have been of service to others. I have gone to therapy. None of these activities has done much to change how I feel.

I am confident now that I cannot think my way out of the place I am in. I have thought without ceasing about the solution to my pain for over thirty years—ad nauseam. I have read the right books and embraced the ideas and philosophies—for a while. The best ideas I have read, or come up with on my own, have done little to change how I feel.

So, if I cannot act my way out of the mind-set, and I cannot think my way out either, what options do I have left? By the way, I have tried to pray my way out, too. Although the benefits of twenty years of meditation are enormous and immeasurable, I still feel pretty much the same way about myself as I did twenty years ago. And how I feel about myself *is* the central issue in my universe. Make no mistake about it, *I am my life's work.* Working on myself is what I have done since I woke up, some time late in my teens.

Now I have come to believe that the process of recovery for me is not based on what I do, and it is not an intellectual process—*for sure* it is not an intellectual process. Thinking takes me off on flights of fancy, and sometimes it feels really good, but it doesn't change me inside.

I believe that there is integrity to my process. I believe that the force inside me that wants to be healthy and free is dominant—much stronger than the forces that have kept me stuck for so long. What then is the solution? I'm not sure—but I have the insights and the help of the author of this book.

I believe now that the solution is simply to sit still, and feel and be aware of what I am feeling *as I am feeling it.* I think if I just get out of my own way, the process (which is already in place and which has integrity) will just take care of itself—and I will be taken care of in the process. The work is much simpler, and much more subtle, than I ever imagined.

As I stated, my primary motivation for all my thoughts and actions has always been to stop the pain I feel. So now when the proposed solution to my pain is *to sit still and feel the pain,* I have a real dilemma. It goes against everything I have taught myself, everything I have been trying to accomplish. And it defies a most basic and natural instinct.

Nothing could be more natural or make more sense than avoiding pain. So in order to embrace this work, a great deal of faith and courage is needed. In my case, the solid belief that this is the right and true process makes the difference, much as the athlete consents to endure physical pain because of the certain knowledge that this is the way to growth and progress.

It is not necessary to believe in order to do this work. I just ruled out every other way by trial and error, and so came to a willingness to believe, and to do the work. The courage came as a by-product of my own desperation and the unquenchable desire for final freedom. The faith came from seeing my friend, Jan, through her process. She paved the way for me, and this book can pave the way for all who can come to this work with hope and courage.

BIBLIOGRAPHY

Among the following publications, those with asterisks (*) are recommended reading.

BRADSHAW, JOHN. *Bradshaw On: The Family.* Deerfield Beach, Fla.: Health Communications, 1988.

BEATTIE, MELODY. *Co-Dependent No More.* New York: Harper/Hazelden, 1982.

CERMAK, TIMMEN L. *Diagnosing and Treating Co-Dependency.* Minneapolis: The Johnson Institute, 1986.

JANOV, ARTHUR, PH.D. *The Primal Scream.* New York: Perigee Books, 1970.

KÜBLER-ROSS, ELISABETH. *On Death and Dying.* New York: Macmillan, 1969.

MELLODY, PIA, MILLER & MILLER. *Facing Co-Dependence.* New York: Harper San Francisco, 1989.

*MILLER, ALICE. *The Drama of the Gifted Child.* New York: Basic Books, 1980.

*————. *For Your Own Good.* New York: Farrar, Straus and Giroux, 1984.

*————. *Thou Shalt Not Be Aware.* New York: Farrar, Straus and Giroux, 1985.

*————. *The Untouched Key.* New York: Doubleday, 1990.

*————. *Banished Knowledge.* New York: Doubleday, 1990.

*————. *Breaking Down the Wall of Silence.* New York: Dutton, 1991.

OLIVER-DIAZ, PHILLIP, AND PATRICIA A. O'GORMAN. *12 Steps to Self-parenting.* Deerfield Beach, Fla: Health Communications, 1988.

POLLARD, JOHN K., III. *Self-parenting.* Malibu Canyon, Calif.: Generic Human Studies Publications, 1987.

RECOVERY PUBLICATIONS. *The 12 Steps for Adult Children.* San Diego: Recovery Publications, 1987.

————. *The 12 Steps—A Way Out.* San Diego: Recovery Publications, 1987.

SCHAEF, ANNE WILSON. *Co-Dependence, Misunderstood, Mistreated.* Minneapolis: Winston Press, 1986.

WEGSCHIEDER-CRUISE, SHARON. *Choicemaking—For Co-dependents, Adult Children, and Spirituality Seekers.* Pompano Beach, Fla.: Health Communications, 1985.

Index